501
Practical
ways to
L♥VE
your Wife
&Kids

501 Practical ways to LOVE your Wife & Kids

By Roger Sonnenberg

CPH.®

SAINT LOUIS

I dedicate this book to those who have taught
me much about what it is to be a father and a
husband and who continue to impact my life
in more ways that they'll ever know:
my wife, Robin,
my son, Jacob,
my parents, Reinhart and Bertha Sonnenberg,
and my wife's parents, Jack and Joyce Ijames.

2   3   4   5   6   7   8   9   10   05 04 03 02 01 00 99 98 97 96

Contents

INTRODUCTION

You will soon discover that this book is arranged chronologically, according to the months of the calendar year. The first chapter has a January theme, the second a February theme, and so forth.

You don't have to wait until January to start reading this book or wait for the start of each new month to begin its corresponding chapter. (But if that's how you want to do it, wonderful!) This book can be read at any time of the year—and at whatever pace you choose. The benefits of reading it go beyond the "order" I have chosen. The value of the ideas expressed doesn't depend on the time or season of the year you read them.

You will find that each chapter ends with a list of suggested activities—some to do on your own, some to do with your wife, some to do with your children, and some to do as a family. There are around 500 activities, so I don't honestly expect you to do them all. The point is, if you can do some of them, or even just a few, you will grow in your role of husband and father, and your family will be enriched because of it. That, at least, is my prayer.

Blessings on your reading!

Celebrate the Future

It was New Year's Eve. Everyone was talking about the new year. Some were making plans to celebrate its arrival with a party. Others were discussing their hopes that this year would be better than the last.

As 5-year-old David listened to the adults, he began thinking about the new year and what it might bring. Looking at his father, he asked, "Dad, will tomorrow really be different?"

Dad didn't know for sure what David was talking about, so he asked, "What do you mean?"

"I just heard some people say that tomorrow would be a brand-new year," David explained. "*Will* it be a brand-new year?"

"Yes," answered his father.

"Well, if it's going to be brand new, does that mean it will be different from today?" inquired David.

———※◦◦※———

As we enter a new year, it's wise to ponder David's question: Will this year be any different from the last? Will we fight the same old battles with our wife? Will we continue the same bad habits that irritate her? Will we make the same silly mistakes in our parenting? Will the new year be a rerun of the old?

The Parable of the Fig Tree

As we look back on the past year, we acknowledge that we have made mistakes. We have sinned against God and others. However, as the parable of the fig tree in Luke 13:6–9 reminds us, the new year need not be a carbon copy of the past year. Year after year, the vineyard owner came seeking some fruit from a carefully tended fig tree. But each year he found the tree barren. Though the tree looked beautiful and healthy, it produced nothing of value. The owner ordered it cut down and replaced with another, but his gardener begged him: "Leave it alone for one more year, and I'll dig around it and fertilize it. If it bears fruit next year, fine! If not, then cut it down" (Luke 13:8–9).

The meaning of the parable is obvious. Jesus was saying that God's people are to bear fruit. And though we do not always produce the kind of fruit God is looking for, He is still gracious and merciful to us. Our Advocate, Jesus Christ, pleads our case before the Father, and we are given a second chance. "Who will bring any charge against [us]? … Christ Jesus, who died—more than that, who was raised to life—is at the right hand of God and is also interceding for us" (Romans 8:33–34). As we feed on His Word and bask in His love and mercy, we can celebrate our future—a future that does not have to be a rerun of the past.

A New Year of Blessings

I pray that you will celebrate this new year in many different ways. Celebrate everything from being more responsible to being more committed. Celebrate traditions. Celebrate service to one another. Celebrate the privilege of prayer and God's gift of your loved ones. Celebrate being a husband and a father!

In their best-selling book *The Blessing*, Gary Smalley and John Trent suggest that there are few things more important to celebrate than when a husband and/or a father gives blessings to his wife and children. To bless means "to invoke divine favor" upon someone. In the Old Testament, the blessing of a family member passed on God's favor, God's approval, and God's promises (see for example, Genesis 28:1–4). In the New Testament, blessing can have a similar meaning (for example, in Luke 1:39–45).

Smalley and Trent identify five basic elements in Old and New Testament blessings that are important for us to incorporate into the blessings we offer others:

1. Meaningful touch.
2. A spoken message.
3. Attaching high value to the one being blessed.
4. Picturing a special future for the one being blessed.
5. An active commitment to fulfill the blessing.[1]

Blessing with Meaningful Touch

The Scriptures are full of examples where touching—including hugging, kissing, and the laying on of hands—

was an important part of blessing someone. Jesus "reached out His hand and touched the [leprous] man. ... He said. 'Be clean!' Immediately the leprosy left him and he was cured" (Mark 1:41–42). Touching a leper was strictly forbidden by Jewish law, but Jesus did it anyway. Imagine the feelings of the leprous man! How he must have yearned for someone to heal him and, yes, even to touch him.

Studies tell us that the average person needs 8 to 10 touches a day to stay physically, emotionally, and spiritually well. Yet a recent survey shows that the average father, for all practical purposes, stops touching his children by the time they reach the age of 8. The same holds true in many marriages. Within a few years after the wedding, spouses tend to decrease their tactile communication, except during sexual intercourse. Meaningful touch is surely one of the best ways we have of expressing our love for one another. Before leaving for work, a father blesses not only himself, but his wife and his children as well, when he remembers to take time to hug and kiss each one good-bye.

In a program developed by the Touch Research Institute, senior citizens acting as surrogate grandparents gave massages to neglected and abused babies in a shelter. As a result, the babies slept better and were more alert, active, and sociable when awake.

But the adults benefited too. They made fewer trips to the doctor's office and spent more time with friends. They reported less anxiety and depression and more self-esteem. Levels of stress-related hormones in their urine decreased too.[2]

Blessing with Meaningful Words

The second element of blessing is that of the spoken word. Words have great power. They can be positive or negative. They can build up or tear down. They can comfort or hurt.

The story of Isaac, Jacob, and Esau (Genesis 27:1–40) offers an example of someone crying out for a blessing of words. Owing to a series of contrived circumstances, Jacob receives the blessing of his father, Isaac, instead of Esau. Isaac affirms Jacob, "Ah, the smell of my son is like the smell of a field that the LORD has blessed" (v. 27). Though such an affirmation today would not seem very complimentary, in that day and age it was. Once Esau learns that Isaac's blessing has gone to his younger brother, he is devastated. "Bless me too, my father!" he cries (v. 38).

Such cries for blessings of affirmation can be heard in many homes today. We all need to know that someone cares. A wife needs to know that she's still attractive to her husband. Children need to know that what they think and feel matters. One way or another, they will seek out those who make them feel important and valuable. That's one reason why children, lacking a better alternative, are attracted to cults and gangs. If a father fails to assure his daughter that she is special and important, she will go elsewhere to hear it.

If anyone can give affirmation, it is the Christian

husband and father. Why? Because that is in keeping with God's plan for our families. Fathers are to be the heads of their families as Jesus is the head of the church (Ephesians 5:21–6:4).

Blessing by Attaching High Value

The third element of blessing is expressing high value. A child needs to know that he or she is important. In God's eyes we are all important—young and old alike—valuable enough for Him to sacrifice His only Son to win our redemption.

We show others how we value them by the way we speak to them and treat them. A husband who tells his wife, "I'm so proud of the way you handle the children" is telling her that she is valuable. A father who asks for his son's opinion on an important question is telling his son that he thinks his opinions are important.

Blessing by Picturing a Special Future

The fourth element of blessing is to picture or envision a special future for the one being blessed. When one pictures a special future for another, it gives that person positive direction. Smalley and Trent state:

> A law of physics says that water cannot rise above its source. ... If a parent pictures for a child that his or her value in life is low, that child will find it difficult to rise above these words. In one insightful study of fathers and their daughters, it was found

*that these women's achievements in life were directly
related to the level of their father's acceptance of
them. Those who truly desire to give their children
the blessing will provide the room for these boys and
girls to grow by encouraging their potential and by
picturing a special future for them.*[3]

The most important hope that every Christian parent
can give to his child is the picture of eternal life through
Jesus Christ. It is a parent's most important privilege and
task because, when the child closes his eyelids in death,
what else really matters but that he knows that Jesus
Christ is his Savior? Paul writes:

> *But our citizenship is in heaven. And we eagerly
> await a Savior from there, the Lord Jesus Christ, who,
> by the power that enables Him to bring everything
> under His control, will transform our lowly bodies so
> that they will be like His glorious body. (Philippians
> 3:20–21)*

Blessing through Active Commitment

The final element of blessing is that of active commitment. This means that one will do more than talk. He
will also walk the walk. God reminds us of this truth in
James 1:23–24:

> *Anyone who listens to the word but does not do
> what it says is like a man who looks at his face in a
> mirror and, after looking at himself, goes away and
> immediately forgets what he looks like.*

A husband must not simply talk about being in love; he must *behave* in love. A father must do more than tell his children that he loves them; he must *demonstrate* that he loves them. He must spend time with them. He must play with them. He must attend their sports banquets and the open house sponsored by the school.

"Bless me too, my father," Esau cried out to Isaac (Genesis 27:38). Esau was not alone in asking for a blessing. *Everyone* asks for blessings, including your wife and children. This year, pledge to bless those you love the most!

➤ Suggestions for Husbands ⭠

Week 1

Be a source of blessing to your wife through meaningful touch.

➤ Embrace your wife today.

➤ Tonight, when you watch TV together, sit next to her and hold hands.

➤ Give her a massage—with no strings attached!

➤ Kiss your wife every morning before you go to work. Believe it or not, a study out of Germany suggests that men who kiss their wives every morning live longer than those who don't.

➤ Give your wife a shoulder rub.

➤ When you talk to your wife, gently touch her to communicate that you care about her.

➤ Lady Chesterfield once said, "My child, if you finally decide to let a man kiss you, put your whole heart into it. No man likes to kiss a rock." Kiss your wife today like you haven't kissed her in a long time, putting "your whole heart into it."

Week 2

Be a source of blessing to your wife by bestowing a meaningful word that expresses the high value you place on her.

➤ Communication is best done before your wife dies (in other words, don't leave things unsaid too long!). Tell your wife you love her and that she means the world to you.

➤ It's not only what one says, rather, it's how one says it that makes all the difference. Make a conscientious effort to say everything you need to say in a loving way.

➤ Good communication requires the sharing of feelings. Make a real effort to share more than facts. Share your feelings as well.

➤ Ask yourself, *What's the thing I love most about my wife?* Once you've sorted through all the different things and chosen just one, tell her what it is.

➤ "Attending behavior" (e.g., eye contact, facial expressions, posture) affects the behavior of another person more than the words themselves. Make a conscientious effort to use "attending behavior" that tells your wife you love her.

➤ Send your wife a special greeting card that conveys your love for her.

➤ Read Philippians 4:8. Then make every effort to praise your wife for one thing she does each day.

Week 3

Be a source of blessing to your wife by picturing a special future for her.

- Review Jeremiah 29:11 with your wife.

- Discuss with her the hopes and dreams you have together for retirement. Be sure to hear your wife's expectations. When you know each other's goals, you are better able to build that future together.

- Talk about heaven. Look up passages in Scripture that speak of heaven. At the end of your discussion, pray together, thanking God for the gift of heaven through Jesus Christ.

- Review Matthew 6:25–34. Reminisce about how God has provided for you in the past. Then thank God that, just as He provided for your yesterdays, so you are confident He will provide for your tomorrows.

- Some people spend their entire lives waiting and waiting for something better, putting their lives on hold. Be grateful to God for what you have today, knowing that no matter what, everything is right between God and you because of Jesus Christ.

Week 4

Be a source of blessing to your wife by not only being in love with her but *behaving* in love.

- Bring your wife some flowers.

- Surprise your wife by doing something you normally would never do, such as clearing the table after dinner.

- Take a walk with your wife and hold her hand.

➤ Review Ephesians 5:25. Then review whether the things you've said or done to your wife are Christ-like. If not, ask your wife's forgiveness and try again!

➤ Go out for dinner—just you and your wife!

➤ Take a drive. Stop at an area motel and rent a room. The rest is up to your imagination.

➤ Plan a surprise weekend getaway. Arrange for baby-sitting. Secretly pack a bag for both of you. When you get home after work, tell your wife to jump in the car and get ready for a wonderful weekend.

❧ Suggestions for Fathers ❧

Week 1

Be a source of blessing for your children through meaningful touch.

➤ Take a walk around the block with each of your children. As you do, hold his or her hand.

➤ Studies show that people need meaningful touch to remain physically, emotionally, and spiritually healthy. Think of ways you can communicate your love for your child through meaningful touch. Then use some of these ways to communicate with your child.

➤ This evening, as you pray with each of your children, hold his or her hand.

➤ Before you leave for work, hug your children.

➤ Make a conscientious effort to gently touch your children as you communicate with them.

➤ Watch a video or a good TV program with your children. Sit next to them or lie on the floor with them—close.

Week 2

Be a source of blessing to your children by bestowing a meaningful word that expresses the high value you place on them.

➤ Commend your children for obeying you.

➤ Encourage them with phrases such as "You're the greatest!" or "You're such a gift from God."

➤ Lower your voice two decibels when reprimanding your children.

➤ Compliment your children.

➤ Review Psalm 139:1–18. Reminisce with your children about how joyful and proud you were when they were born and the expectations you had and have for them.

➤ Ask yourself how healthy your children would be if their health depended on your loving words. Make the appropriate changes to ensure your children's "good health."

Week 3

Be a source of blessing to your children by picturing a special future for them.

➤ Review Jeremiah 29:11 with your children. Ask what they think the verse means for them.

➤ The writer of Proverbs reminds us, "As [man] thinketh in his heart, so is he" (23:7 KJV). *By your statements, what kind of future are you picturing for your children?*

➤ Review with your children John 3:16. Then rejoice and thank God for the special future He has in store for His people.

➤ Talk with your children about what they would like to be someday. Encourage them in their dreams.

➤ Talk to your children about their special God-given gifts. Then talk about why God has given these special gifts to them and how they can be used in the future (e.g., in the profession they choose).

Week 4

Be a source of blessing to your children by not only talking about your love but showing it through your actions.

➤ Spend some extra time with your children.

➤ Go out for dinner together, just you and your child.

➤ Show your children that you love them enough to discipline them.

➤ Ask your children what they would like to do. Then, if appropriate, do it with them.

➤ Cancel one of your important appointments to spend extra time with your children, doing what they enjoy.

➤ Go fishing with your children.

CELEBRATE LOVE

The dry goods merchant F. W. Woolworth opened his first store in a small town. His arrival was anything but appreciated by another merchant down the street whose family-owned store had been in business for decades. As Woolworth's grand opening drew near, his long-established rival placed the following ad in the local paper:

Do your business here!
We've been in business for 50 years!

Young Woolworth wasn't daunted. He simply countered with the following ad the next week:

Our store has been
in business only a week!
All of our merchandise is brand new!

Business boomed for Woolworth. People liked the idea of new merchandise. Sometimes things do get old. Merchandise can get old—food, clothing, furniture. So can love!

Valentine Love

February 14th is a day for sweethearts to reflect on their love for one another. Often they exchange Valentine cards. A husband might take his wife out for dinner or bring home flowers. Or both!

According to legend, the celebration of Valentine's Day originated with a man named Valentine. Saint Valentine, an early Christian, lived in Rome in the third century—a time when Christians were often imprisoned and put to death for their faith in Jesus Christ. Valentine himself would meet such a fate. One story has it that shortly after being thrown into prison, he fell in love with the jailer's daughter, who happened to be blind. He prayed daily for her eyesight to be restored. His prayers were answered in the affirmative: she received her sight. Just before Valentine was executed, he sent a love note to the girl, reiterating his love for her. He signed the note simply, "From your Valentine." Thus, we celebrate Valentine's Day, a day reserved for personal expressions of love.

A Congregation Whose Love Grew Old

Jesus spoke of deteriorating love in the book of Revelation. He noted that the church of Ephesus, the largest church in Asia, had forsaken its first love—its Bridegroom, Jesus Himself (Revelation 2:4). It had fallen out of love.

The bride, the people of the Ephesian congregation, had originally been very much in love with the Groom, Jesus Christ. They had demonstrated their love for Him, and Jesus had commended their fidelity:

"I know your deeds, your hard work and your perseverance. I know that you cannot tolerate wicked men, that you have tested those who claim to be apostles but are not, and have found them false. You have persevered and have endured hardships for My name, and have not grown weary." (Revelation 2:2–3)

However, something happened to the bride's love for the Lord. It grew pale, losing its vibrancy and luster. He warned her of dire consequences if she didn't change. "If you do not repent, I will come to you and remove your lampstand from its place" (Revelation 2:5).

Despite the bride's unfaithfulness, the Bridegroom, Jesus, was faithful, patient, and understanding. In verse 5, He succinctly spells out a plan to help her fall back in love:

1. *Remember:* "Remember the height from which you have fallen!"

2. *Repent:* "Repent."

3. *Redo:* "And do the things you did at first."

Reviewing this three-point prescription can help us not only fall back in love with God but also with one another.

Remember

Jesus tells us to "remember the height from which you have fallen" (Revelation 2:5). In what ways have you fallen out of love with your wife? What was it like when you were first married? Do you remember how you laughed together about the silliest things? how you talked to one another for hours? how you couldn't say "I love you" often enough?

> *Eddie Cantor was a famous radio entertainer in the 1930's. One of his popular songs was entitled "Ida," named after his beloved wife. He often spent long periods of time away from his family in order to further his career. He recalled his mother telling him: "Eddie, don't go too fast or you will miss the scenery." One day the truthfulness of that statement came crashing in on him. After the grand opening of a new show he received a telegram: "Ida just gave birth to your fourth daughter." All he could think of was his mother's statement: "Eddie, don't go too fast or you will miss the scenery." "That's exactly what's happening!" Eddie exclaimed, "I'm going too fast. I'm missing the scenery."[4]*

Do you remember the promises you made to yourself—and to your wife—when your first child was born? All the good times you'd have with him? All the promises you made that you'd never be like *your* dad, putting your work first? What's happened to those promises?

Husbands and wives often concentrate on all the things that are wrong in their relationship, failing to count the things that are right. Because of this, they claim they've grown apart. Some even say it was a mistake to get married in the first place, that they never really loved each other at all. Such thinking is the result of selective memory. Studies show that people often remember only those events and experiences that are congruent with their present way of thinking. If they think everything is wrong with their marriage, they'll selectively recall those things that were wrong in their marriage's earlier stage and forget about the things that were and are still right. Jesus is telling the people of Ephesus and us: *Remember what it used to be like!* Relive the way it used to be before your marriage started drifting. Relive the time when you first loved.

The singer-songwriter Tom T. Hall recalled an interview he once heard on a radio talk show. A psychiatrist said that the way to have a good day was to sit down first thing every morning and make a list of everything and everyone you dislike. By writing these things down on paper and then throwing the paper away, you could get rid of your grievances for the day. "That," Hall said, "seemed too negative. I couldn't see starting my day off by thinking of all those ugly things. It seemed better to think of happy things, things I loved. So I made a list, and part of that list became a song, "I Love."

In the song, Hall lists the things he loves most, from the simplest things to the more profound, periodically adding the words "And I love you." A long list of happy things that you remember about your wife can do much more good for your marriage than a long list of things that are wrong.

Repent

The next step in falling back in love is to repent of the things you have said or done that have hurt your relationship with your wife or your children. This repentance needs to be void of excuses. It calls for making an honest survey of the way you have treated your family.

- ❏ Have I placed unrealistic expectations on my wife or children?
- ❏ Have I loved my family as Christ loves me?
- ❏ Have I been disrespectful to them?
- ❏ Have I taken my frustrations from work out on them?
- ❏ Have I belittled them in front of other people?
- ❏ Have I spoken to them in an unkind way?
- ❏ Have I been patient with them?
- ❏ Have I lied to them?
- ❏ Have I thought evil of them?
- ❏ Have I spoken the truth to them in love?

It helps to confess your shortcomings—both to yourself and to God. Figure out what it is that's keeping you from being the kind of husband and father God wants you to be. Move the roadblocks that are keeping you from being a Christlike husband and father.

God assures us that as we confess these sins, He will forgive us: "If we confess our sins, He is faithful and just and will forgive us our sins and purify us from all unrighteousness" (1 John 1:9). With Jesus' precious blood, God washes away our sins without a trace. In this forgiveness, we are restored to new life.

Unfortunately, in many marriages, one or both of the partners doesn't think it's possible to change. To say you can't change, to say you can't fall back in love, is to say that God's love is not powerful enough to make that happen. To say you or your wife cannot change is to deny the resurrection power that is yours through your Baptism:

> *I pray also that the eyes of your heart may be enlightened in order that you may know the hope to which He has called you, the riches of His glorious inheritance in the saints, and His incomparably great power for us who believe. That power is like the working of His mighty strength, which He exerted in Christ when He raised Him from the dead. (Ephesians 1:18–20)*

———◆———

A. C. Green, power forward for the Phoenix Suns basketball team, shares in his book *Victory* the following keys for winning a spiritual war:

1. ***Know you have an enemy.*** *No matter how you slice it, you're at war. ... It's the devil. ... He doesn't like you, and he is actively trying to defeat you.*

2. ***Understand your enemy.*** *Every basketball player can be thrown off his game by opponents who learn his weakness. In a similar way, the enemy knows your weaknesses and he's prepared to exploit them.*

3. ***Know your teammates.*** *Who is on your side? ... Besides the people, know the Bible. You have to believe it by faith, confess it and meditate on it*

until it comes alive inside you. The Bible is a weapon. But it's only a lethal weapon when it's in your heart and spirit. Get the words off the page and into your heart.

4. **Use your arsenal.** *You have the power of the Word, … and the gifts of the Holy Spirit: self-control, wisdom and discernment. Discernment is spiritual understanding. In basketball we develop a nose for the ball, knowing which way it will come off the rim for a rebound. In spiritual warfare, discernment gives you that nose for the enemy, understanding in your spirit what he's up to before your mind can even grasp it.*[5]

Redo

Finally, Jesus tells us to "do the things you did at first" (Revelation 2:5). This means courting your wife again. Bring her candy or flowers or whatever it was in the early days that she liked so much. Go out for dinner and talk, looking each other in the eyes. Woo her. Call her in the middle of the day just to say you're thinking about her. Make a conscious decision to put the spark back in your marriage.

Many people define love as something one feels emotionally—a "snap, crackle, and pop" kind of thing! Counselors often hear clients say, "I just don't feel in love with her anymore!" or "I don't feel like making love to him." In reality, these people are saying, "If I feel a certain way, then I'll react in a certain way." Well, it can work the other way too. *Doing* certain things can *revitalize* even the most lifeless marriage.

More Than Feeling

O God
If You've taught us any one lesson
In our years of marriage
It is simply this:
Love is so much more than feeling. ...

How do we know?
We know because despite
Our varying emotions
Despite our wounded egos
We've given ourselves
In a deliberate act of will
"Till death do us part."
That was our solemn commitment!
It is this very commitment
That forever sustains our love.[6]

At the wedding in Cana (John 2:1–11), the host suddenly found himself in a real fix: he had run out of wine for his guests. Noting this, Mary, Jesus' mother, asked her son to help. Our Lord complied. He took several empty jars, ordered them filled with water, and then miraculously turned that water into wine—wine far superior, by the way, to the wine originally served by the host.

Jesus is more than capable of doing this very sort of thing with our depleted or worn-out marriages. The servants at the Cana wedding did what Jesus told them to do. So we also must obey His instructions as the Holy Spirit helps us restock the wine supply in our marriages: "Remember the height from which you have fallen! Repent and do the things you did at first" (Revelation 2:5).

⤜ Suggestions for Husbands ⤛

Week 1

Compare your love for your wife with the description of love in 1 Corinthians 13:4–13.

➤ Does your love include the various aspects of love enumerated in this passage? Mark an × under the heading that best describes you. Ask your wife to complete the grid as well. Compare answers.

➤ Memorize 1 Corinthians 13:4–8a.

➤ Pray the following prayer with your wife:
Lord God, enable us to love each other with agape love, a God-given love. Give us the love described by St. Paul in 1 Corinthians 13:

a love that is patient,
a love that is kind,
a love that does not envy,
a love that does not boast,
a love that does not get proud,
a love that is not rude,
a love that is not self-seeking,

God's Definition of Love	I have no problem in this aspect of love.		I occasionally have problems in this aspect of love.		I frequently have problems in this aspect of love.		I need work on this aspect of love.	
	Him	Her	Him	Her	Him	Her	Him	Her
Patient								
Kind								
Not jealous								
Not boastful/ conceited								
Not indecent/ ill-mannered								
Not selfish								
Not easily angered								
Not harmful								
Not delighting in evil but good								
Bears everything								
Believes everything								
Hopes for everything								
Endures everything								
Never dies								

a love that is not easily angered,
a love that keeps no record of wrongs,
a love that does not delight in evil
    but rejoices with the truth.

Give us Jesus' love, a love
that always protects,
that always trusts,
that always hopes,
that always perseveres.

Give us a love for our spouse that never fails.
In Jesus' name. Amen.

➤ With your wife, practice the giving and receiving of love by doing the following exercise.

1. Set aside some time when the two of you will be undisturbed. Each of you write down three or four things you love about your spouse. Be specific (e.g., "I love the way you kiss me when you come home from work").

2. Upon completing your lists, takes turns sharing them. Do this by going behind your partner, putting your hands on her (his) shoulders, and telling her (him) the things you love about her (him).

3. After each of you has taken your turn, talk about which was easier, the giving or the receiving.

- Serve your wife breakfast in bed. Make her feel like she's been chosen "Mrs. America" or "Queen for a Day."

- Prepare a bubble bath for your wife. While she's taking her bath, serve her cheese and crackers and her favorite beverage.

Week 2

Concentrate on the first part of the instructions in Revelation 2:5: "Remember the height from which you have fallen!"

- Compare your love for your wife with the love Jesus shows to us (see Luke 15:11–32; John 3:16; Romans 5:6–8).

- With your wife, recall your courtship days. Remember the times you laughed together, the communication that took place, the dinners you ate together. If you've stopped courting your wife, why have you?

- Spend time with your wife looking over your wedding pictures or watching your wedding video. Share with each other what you felt on that day.

- Phone your wife from work and ask her out for dinner and a movie. Remember how you used to do it.

- Review Philippians 4:8. Make a list of all the things you love about your wife and share them with her.

Week 3

Concentrate on the second part of the instructions in Revelation 2:5: "Repent."

➤ Think of how you have hurt your wife with your *words* and ask God for forgiveness.

➤ Think of how you have hurt your wife with your *actions* and ask God for forgiveness.

➤ Think of *promises* you have made to your wife and broken. Ask God for forgiveness.

➤ Relationships are healthiest when there is heart-to-heart sharing. This includes an honest sharing of any wrongdoing or hurtful thing done against each other. The following exercise will stimulate such heart-to-heart sharing.

1. Choose an appropriate time to share with one another.

2. Begin by confessing things you have done that have hurt your relationship (e.g., become jealous). Stop yourself from making excuses, shifting responsibility, or blaming.

3. Ask forgiveness of your wife.

4. Once confession has been made, your wife has the privilege of announcing forgiveness: "Know you are forgiven because of the life, death, and resurrection of our Savior, Jesus Christ. He forgives you, and I do too."

5. Reverse roles and hear your wife's confession and assure her of forgiveness.

6. Close with prayer, especially asking that God might change each of you in ways that will improve your relationship.[7]

➤ François de La Rochefoucauld wrote, "We pardon in the degree that we love." Today, whenever you feel anger, bitterness, or resentment, pray this simple prayer: "Lord, increase my love! Amen."

Week 4

Concentrate on the last part of the instructions in Revelation 2:5: "Do the things you did at first."

➤ Bring home some flowers.

➤ Plan a date. Do what you did when you courted her. Come home and take a shower, shave, put on lots of cologne, and get into your car. Drive around the block a few times. Stop in front of the house. Walk up the sidewalk and ring the doorbell. Let her greet you at the door and chat for a while. Then go to the movies or out for dinner. Take her to that favorite parking place over the city or wherever! When you get home, walk her to the door and kiss her goodnight. Get back in your car and drive it into the garage. The point is this: Do what you once did! Open the doors. Pull out the chair. Bring the flowers or candy. Be as romantic as you used to be!

➤ Communicate at the dinner table tonight, making sure you look each other in the eyes.

➤ Call her in the middle of your work day and tell her you've been thinking about her.

➤ Eat out at a totally new restaurant and order something you've never tried before.

➤ Invite your wife to join you in a new hobby or activity, such as line dancing, running, or bird-watching.

❯❯ Suggestions for Fathers ❮❮

Week 1

Compare your love for your children with the description of agape love in 1 Corinthians 13.

➤ Reread 1 Corinthians 13. As you think about your love for your children, how does it compare with the description in 1 Corinthians 13:4–8?

➤ Discuss 1 Corinthians 13 with your children. Challenge them to memorize as much of this chapter as they can.

➤ Each day, take one of the many descriptions of love from 1 Corinthians 13:4–8 and work on it. For example, one day, work on the description "Love is kind." Do kind things for your children, such as taking time off from work to play in the backyard with your kids.

➤ Read *The Velveteen Rabbit* to your children. Explain that love is costly. Finally, recall the great price that God paid for His love for us—He gave His only-begotten Son to die for us (John 3:16; 1 John 3:16).

➤ Take a large piece of butcher paper or poster board and cut out a heart that measures at least 2′ by 5′. Place the heart somewhere you and your family pass by often, like the refrigerator. Write "Love is …" on the heart and throughout the week use magic markers to write statements that complete the phrase. Do it whenever you've felt loved by your wife, your children, or others. For example, after receiving a hug, you might write, "Love is ... receiving a special hug from your daughter!" Some of the statements may sound silly, but that's okay. Make sure all your children add their definitions.

Week 2

Concentrate on the first part of the instructions in Revelation 2:5: "Remember the height from which you have fallen!"

➤ Study Deuteronomy 8:1–20.

➤ Look at the earliest pictures or videos you took of your children. As you look at the pictures, recall how you felt and what kinds of dreams and hopes you had for your children.

➤ Recall why you named each child as you did. Sit down and explain to them why their names were and are special to you.

➤ List values your parents taught you and the techniques they used in teaching these values. Then ask yourself which of these values you want to teach your children and how you're going to do it.

➤ Recall a time when you received special recognition from your parents for something you did. *How did it make you feel?* Recognize your children in a special way for something they have done.

Week 3

Concentrate on the second part of the instructions in Revelation 2:5: "Repent."

➤ Tell your children you're sorry for something you did that was wrong.

➤ At the dinner table, include a special petition asking God's forgiveness for the things you did that hurt others.

➤ Talk to your children about the meaning of the petition in the Lord's Prayer that reads, "And forgive us our trespasses as we forgive those who trespass against us."

➤ Ask your children how you've hurt them over the last week. Don't argue. Just listen to what they say. Then ask for their forgiveness for those things you said or did that were wrong.

➤ Study Luke 15:11–32. Explain to your children that no matter what they might do someday, you will always love them. You may not like or approve of their actions, but you will always love them as your special son or daughter.

Week 4

Concentrate on the last part of the instructions in Revelation 2:5: "Do the things you did at first."

➤ Read a story to your children like you used to when they were younger.

➤ When you communicate with your children, lovingly touch them.

➤ Remind yourself of your children's frailty by posting a sign in your bathroom: *Children Are Fragile: Handle with Care.*

➤ Spend some extra time with your children today. Remember, your children are young for only a short while.

➤ Treat your children as you like to be treated.

➤ Look at your children's hands. They're small. Don't expect perfection from them.

➤ Take a walk with your children, going at their pace instead of yours. Remember, they have shorter legs than you do.

CELEBRATE PRAYER

Richard Foster in his book *Prayer* tells the story of a man who took his 2-year-old son to the shopping mall. Shortly after arriving at the mall, the child began throwing a tantrum, screaming at the top of his lungs. Concerned shoppers looked at the father, almost as if they were questioning whether he was provoking the child or simply lacked the capability to care for him.

Nothing the father did seemed to help until he picked up his son, held him close to his chest, and started to sing a song, making up the tune and the words as he went along. "I love you. I love you. I'm so glad you're my son. You make me so happy." His singing was off key, but it didn't matter to the child. He was calmed by it.

The father continued singing all the way through the mall and out to the car. As he strapped his boy into his car seat, the child looked at him and said, "Daddy, sing it again … again, Daddy … sing it again!"[8]

This story illustrates what happens when God speaks to us in His Word, such as when we hear His Word proclaimed in hymns, and when we respond in prayer. As God speaks to us through His Word and we respond, a great bonding takes place. God scoops us up into His arms, holds us close to His chest, and sings to us. His song is one of love, one that tells us He's glad we're His son or daughter. Through our prayers, we tell Him that we love Him and that we're so happy He's our heavenly Father! And the more we commune with Him, the more we request as did the child of his earthly father, "Daddy, sing it again … again, Daddy … sing it again!"

A Gallup Poll asked the question
"Do you ever pray to God?"

88 percent said yes.
11 percent said no.[9]

March (or any month, for that matter!) is a great month to spend time settling into the arms of God and singing together, communing with the one who is the Giver of all good things, the one who keeps His every promise, the one who says, "Ask and it will be given to you" (Luke 11:9). We often hear that "March comes in like a lion and goes out like a lamb." In many parts of the country, the first part of March is blustery, but the last part is warm and comfy.

You may feel as if you've marched into the month of March with lots of blustery concerns and problems. God's assurance is that with every winter, there's a spring. With every no, there's a yes. With every dead end, there's an open door. Spring is peeking around the corner, reminding us that winter is ending. "See! The winter is past; the rains are over and gone. Flowers appear on the earth; the season of singing has come, the cooing of doves is heard in our land" (Song of Songs 2:11–12).

Our Example—Jesus

Between our Lord's final instructions to His disciples in the Upper Room and His arrest, He communed with God in the Garden of Gethsemane. He was about to die for the sins of the world. All the sins of humanity for all time were being placed upon Him. He would be incapable of bearing the load unless He was strengthened by His heavenly Father. He threw Himself into His Father's arms, saying: "My Father, if it is possible, may this cup be taken from Me. Yet not as I will, but as You will" (Matthew 26:39). As Jesus requested, the Father gave Him the strength He needed to carry the world's sins to the cross.

Through Jesus' example, we see that our strength also comes from God the Father. "If God is for us, who can be against us?" the apostle Paul asks. Then he assures us, "He who did not spare His own Son, but gave Him up for us all—how will He not also, along with Him, graciously give us all things?" (Romans 8:31–32).

———

For 40 minutes, UCLA jumped and bumped against defending national champion Arkansas. UCLA came into the game as the underdog. Many of the UCLA players were young and inexperienced compared to the tougher, older Arkansas Razorbacks. Cameron Dollar, the UCLA sophomore who had to stand in for injured senior point guard Tyus Edney, played almost flawlessly. When it was all over, UCLA had its first NCAA title since 1975 with an 89-78 victory. Coaches and players were shaking their heads in amazement. One coach said, "It was a bit of divine intervention."

After the game, UCLA assistant coach Lorenzo Romar did what he had done many times with the team—he collected the players and together they prayed. The television commentators were at a loss for words. It was a highly unusual occurrence in the sports world. Not, however, for the victorious UCLA basketball team. They had done it throughout the season—through defeat and victory!

ACTS

Prayer is a privilege that God gives to us as Christians. He invites us to come to Him without fear or intimidation. It is God's gift to His people, to families, to husbands and wives. Teaching your children how to pray is one of the most important things you can do for them. Few other forms of communication will help your children more than knowing how to pray. Like other spiritual disciplines—fasting, meditation, confession, and forgiveness—prayer must be practiced. One effective way to help adults and children pray is to practice praying using the acronym ACTS:

A—Adoration
C—Confession
T—Thanksgiving
S—Supplication

Adoration

Adoration is not something that comes automatically—like asking for things. Our children demonstrate this truth when we go to the store with them. They find it easy to ask for this, that, and the other thing. However, to offer up adoration is quite another story. *Adore* means "to worship" or "to show high regard." The Scriptures are filled with words of adoration for God: "Great is the LORD, and most worthy of praise, in the city of our God, His holy mountain" (Psalm 48:1).

C. S. Lewis suggests that adoration is learned from experiencing the ordinary, simple pleasures of life. He calls it the "adoration in infinitesimals." As parents, we often hurry through life and fail to appreciate the infinitesimals, such as the fragrance of roses or the pleasure of feeling our child's tiny hand in ours as we take an evening walk around the block. "To experience the tiny theophany is itself to adore," to adore the Giver of pleasures, God Himself.[10]

Paul echoes the same thought:

> *Finally, brothers, whatever is true, whatever is noble, whatever is right, whatever is pure, whatever is lovely, whatever is admirable—if anything is excellent or praiseworthy—think about such things. … And the God of peace will be with you. (Philippians 4:8–9)*

Confession

After David had committed adultery with Bathsheba and had her husband, Uriah, killed in battle, Nathan confronted David with his sin: "You are the man!" (2 Samuel 12:7). Only after David confessed his sin could healing begin. Sin keeps us from the abundant life God wants for His people. When we make excuses in an attempt to justify our sin—such as, "It wasn't my fault!" or "Everyone else is doing it!"—we keep ourselves from seeing reality and distance ourselves from God. Reality is only recognized and experienced when we are honest with God, others, and ourselves. The early church father Augustine wrote, "The confession of evil works is the first beginning of good works."

Few things hurt families more than when there is an unforgiving spirit within the home or when nobody is ever wrong about anything. Children learn to confess and admit wrongdoing when they see their parents do the same, when they hear daddy say, "I'm sorry, honey" or "Daughter, I was wrong, forgive me."

Thanksgiving

Paul tells us to "give thanks in all circumstances" (1 Thessalonians 5:18). Christians are able to do this because they live with an awareness of God's daily care, even in times of difficulty. The Old Testament patriarch Joseph vividly reminds us of this truth. Joseph's brothers, envious of Joseph, sold him into slavery and told their father that he had died. Later, realizing their sin, they approached Joseph and begged for forgiveness. He replied: "Don't be afraid. Am I in the place of God? You intended to harm me, but God intended it for good to accomplish what is now being done, the saving of many lives" (Genesis 50:19–20).

Paul admonished the Romans: "Therefore let us stop passing judgment on one another" (Romans 14:13). The author Catherine Marshall suggests fasting as a way to concentrate on giving thanks. But before you lock the refrigerator doors, she wants us to abstain from complaining, not food. During the fast, try not to criticize anybody about anything. Instead, reflect on those things that are praiseworthy. Instead of grumbling about the work you have to do, thank God you *have* work to do.

In the powerful film *The Estate Sale,* one of the characters reminisces about how she raised her children.

> *"I rushed through life … the children were grown before I knew it. … I just want to live one day over again, an ordinary day, a day with my children little again, with problems, the washing, cooking, cleaning. … I'd love to do all the things I used to complain about. Just one day. I have so much to tell them."*

Thanksgiving begins by appreciating even the cleaning, washing, and cooking!

Supplication

Dietrich Bonhoeffer, the German Christian apologist and martyr, said, "Intercessory prayer is the purifying bath into which the individual and the fellowship must enter every day." Our problem is that we become so infatuated with ourselves that we often don't think about others, especially enough to pray for them. And yet Scripture repeatedly tells us to pray for one another. "Pray for each other. ... The prayer of a righteous man is powerful and effective" (James 5:16). Intercessory prayer gives us an opportunity to love others, to become intimately involved in building them up, to help them face difficulties as well as celebrate God's love and care.

Praying together binds families to God as well as to one another. Parents are wise in asking their children, "What would you like to pray for today?" Once parents find out, they then pray for their children, incorporating these petitions into their personal prayers. Parents teach a lesson no words can communicate when their children see Mom and Dad praying together, including open and honest confession.

In this month of lion-like beginnings and, one hopes, lamb-like endings, practice the gift of prayer.

———◦◦◦———

"Cover yourself in daily prayer. It doesn't matter when you have devotions. Don't be legalistic about it. It's quality, not quantity, that counts. Let the Holy Spirit guide you."[11]

❧ Suggestions for Husbands ❦

Week 1

This week, concentrate on the A—adoration—in the acronym ACTS. Praise God for who He is—eternal, unchangeable, all-powerful, all-knowing, omnipresent, etc. Remember, God is pleased with the "sacrifice of praise" (Hebrews 13:15).

➤ Sit with your wife and adore God by reading a favorite psalm (see Psalm 23, 91, 96, 145, or 146).

➤ Pray with your wife every day this week. Include the different elements of the acronym ACTS.

➤ Look up the meaning of *adoration* in the dictionary. Ask God to help you have such adoration, not only for God, but for your wife as well. Then do one very specific thing this week that shows how you adore both your Lord and your wife.

➤ Take a walk with your wife and enjoy the infinitesimals along the way, thanking God for these small blessings.

➤ Invite your wife to sit with you and listen together to Handel's *Messiah*.

Week 2

This week, concentrate on the C—confession—in the acronym ACTS. Repeat what God already knows and ask Him for forgiveness. Confess the sins you have committed in thought, word, and deed, not only against God, but against others as well.

➤ Make a conscientious effort to say "I'm sorry" when you've hurt your wife with words or actions. Besides saying it with words, say it with your eyes. Finally, confess it to God and ask for His forgiveness.

➤ Study different confessions recorded in Scripture: Psalm 32; Psalm 51; Daniel 9:3–10. Then speak one of the confessions as your own.

➤ Share with your wife a sin that's been particularly bothersome to you in the last few weeks and that you feel has caused problems in your relationship. Ask for her forgiveness. Also, solicit her prayers in asking God to help you overcome the problems this sin has caused.

➤ Dietrich Bonhoeffer wrote:

> *Our brother ... has been given to us to help us. He hears the confession of our sins in Christ's stead and he forgives our sins in Christ's name. He keeps the secret of our confession as God keeps it. When I go to my brother to confess, I am going to God.*[12]

Ask your wife to hear your confession and to forgive you in Jesus' name, remembering the words of John 20:23: "If you forgive anyone his sins, they are forgiven; if you do not forgive them, they are not forgiven."

➤ Pray that you will take responsibility this week for

your sins instead of denying your wrongdoing or shifting responsibility. Avoid such excuses as "I couldn't help it!" or "Everyone is doing it!"

Week 3

This week, concentrate on the T—thanksgiving—in the acronym ACTS. Thank God for the specific things He has done for you.

➤ For every complaint you have this week, think of at least five things you are grateful for.

➤ Study examples of thanksgiving in the Scriptures: Psalm 16, 23, 118.

➤ Examine different promises given in God's Word, and give thanks for each one (e.g., Psalm 23:1; Isaiah 41:10; John 16:33; 1 Corinthians 10:13; Philippians 4:13; Hebrews 13:6).

➤ Either in your family or personal prayers this week, thank God for your wife and the many qualities that make her special.

➤ Brainstorm different ways to give thanks. For starters, read Exodus 15 and see how Moses and Miriam gave thanks.

➤ Review your prayers. Is the following statement correct about how you often pray? "The mistake a lot of people make when they pray is putting in too many commercials." If so, resolve to change that!

Week 4

This week, concentrate on the S—supplication—in the acronym ACTS. Pray specifically for your own needs as well as the needs of others.

➤ Each morning, ask your wife what special challenges she's going to be facing that day. Then assure her you'll pray that she can successfully meet those challenges. Be sure your promise is carried out—pray!

➤ Pray for your wife each day using the scriptural prayer of Paul: "I pray also that the eyes of [_____'s] heart may be enlightened in order that [she] may know the hope to which [God] has called [her], the riches of His glorious inheritance in the saints, and His incomparably great power for us who believe" (Ephesians 1:18–19).

➤ Pray for your needs and the needs of your wife by using the first part of the common table prayer: "Come, Lord Jesus, be [my/her] guest [add the appropriate ending]

❖ as I meet with my boss."

❖ as she talks to Jimmy's teacher."

❖ as she drives to her parents' home."

➤ After work, spend a 10-and-10 time with your wife. Let her share for 10 minutes what she did during the day, including both her joys and frustrations. Then talk for 10 minutes about your day. Afterward, pray together. Include in your prayers some of the joys and concerns mentioned in your 10-and-10 communication with one another.

➤ Scan the newspaper. Select two or three special needs that surface from the articles, and then pray about them (e.g., the escalation of gang violence).

➤ Review your personal prayers. Could this statement be made about some or even most of your prayers? "Prayer is talking something over with God, rather than trying to talk God out of something!"

❧ Suggestions for Fathers ❧

Week 1

Help your children learn the meaning of adoration, and then lead them in giving God adoration.

➤ If your children are young enough to enjoy such a thing, make a fort out of a card table by placing a blanket over it. Then invite them to crawl in with you and play. Use your imagination. In your conversation and play, remind your children that God is like a fort, a place of refuge (Psalm 9:9; 11:1; 59:16; 71:1).

➤ Crown your child "King for the Evening" by placing a paper crown on him and telling him that for one evening he is king. Let your son decide what he would like to eat and do during the evening (within reason, of course). After his reign, talk to him about how it felt. Was it hard being king? What was fun about it? Then talk to your son about the *real* King, Jesus Christ. Read verses from the book of Revelation that announce that Jesus is "King of kings" (see Revelation 17:14; 19:16). Close with prayer, giving God adoration for being King of your life. (If you have more than one child, make sure each one has a turn being "King [or Queen] for the Evening.")

➤ Sing together the first stanza of "Oh, Come, All Ye Faithful."

"Oh, come, all ye faithful,
Joyful and triumphant!

Oh, come ye, oh, come ye to Bethlehem;
Come and behold Him
Born the king of angels:
Oh, come, let us adore Him,
Oh, come, let us adore Him,
Oh, come, let us adore Him,
Christ the Lord!

➤ Role-play a counseling session. Ask your child to pretend to be the counselor. You pretend to be the client with some problem. Ask your child to help you with some wise advice. Describe how you're feeling. After some time, read Isaiah 9:6; 28:29; and James 1:5. Call attention to the reference to Jesus as our Counselor and the one who gives wisdom. Talk about God being the best of all counselors. Explain that prayer is like a counseling session. We talk to God, and through such talk, we are helped.

• Explain to your child that the meaning of *adore* is "to show high regard." Play a game to see who can think of the most reasons why one should show high regard to God.

Week 2

This week, help your child see the importance of confessing his or her sins.

➤ Explain the meaning of *confess* to your child. Literally, it means "to say the same thing," the same thing that God already knows! Is it scary to know that God knows everything about us? If He does, how can He still love us? Assure your child that, as Christians, we don't have to be afraid because Jesus died and rose to win forgiveness for us.

➤ Read Hebrews 4:15–16. Let your child know that because Jesus was "tempted in every way, just as we are," we can be totally honest with Him. We can say what we're thinking and feeling. Talk about some of the feelings people have—happiness, anger, sadness, depression—and assure your child that God knows how we feel and that He is our best friend. God never divulges any secrets we tell Him. He can be trusted totally!

➤ Assure your children that whenever they ask for forgiveness, the Lord will hear them and forgive them.

➤ Role-play the parable of the two sons (Luke 15:11–32). Note how forgiving the father was. Make sure your child knows that the father in the parable represents God. Celebrate God's forgiveness through Jesus Christ. As a grand finale, go out and celebrate with a huge chocolate sundae or another favorite treat.

➤ Make a conscientious effort to teach confession by your own example. In your prayers with your child, confess your sins and ask God for forgiveness. After you've confessed your sins, thank God for forgiving you.

Week 3

This week remind your children of the many reasons they have for being thankful and the many different ways they can offer thanks to God.

➤ Study the story of the 10 lepers in Luke 17:11–19. Then join hands and give thanks for the blessings you enjoy as a family, asking each person to share the reasons why he or she is thankful.

➤ As a family project, make special prayer reminders for each member of the family. Wrap a small, smooth rock in a cloth bag. Print the following poem on a sheet of paper and attach it to the ribbon holding the bag closed.

> I'm your little prayer rock
> and this is what I'll do …
> Just put me on your pillow
>   till the day is through
> Then turn back the covers
>   and climb into your bed
> And *whack* your little prayer rock
>   will hit you in the head.
> Then you will remember
>   as the day is through
> to kneel and say your prayers
>   as you wanted to.
> Then when you are finished
>   just dump me on the floor
> I'll stay there through nighttime
>   to give you help once more.

When you get up next morning
>   *clunk*, I stub your toe
So you will remember your
>   morning prayers before you go.
Put me back upon your pillow
>   when your bed is made
And your clever little prayer rock
>   will continue in your aid.
Because your heavenly Father
>   cares and loves you so
He wants you to remember
>   to talk to Him, you know.[13]

Give one bag to each member of the family to place on his or her pillow. Then speak a quick prayer of thanks for the privilege of prayer.

➤ Remind your children that one who does not pray when the sun shines may not know how to pray when the clouds come.

➤ Sing the chorus to "When upon Life's Billows," and then spend some time with your children counting your blessings.

>   Count your many blessings—
>   name them one by one,
>   And it will surprise you
>   what the Lord has done.[14]

➤ Each night before you send your children to bed, speak a prayer with them, thanking God for them.

Week 4

This week, teach your children the importance of remembering their own needs as well as the needs of others in prayer.

➤ Each day before you go to work, ask your children what special challenges or needs they'll face that day. Tell them you'll pray for them. More importantly, make sure you *do* pray!

➤ With your child, pray for your pastor, your child's Sunday school teacher, and other church leaders.

➤ With your child, pray that your neighbors will one day be in heaven with you.

➤ As you pray with your children this week, pray that they will someday find a Christian husband or wife (it makes no difference how old the children are).

➤ Teach your children that nothing is too big or too small to pray for. Let them know that God is big enough to be concerned about every detail in life.

➤ As you listen to the evening news and hear something especially sad or happy, ask your family to pray with you about it.

CELEBRATE FORGIVENESS

Easter is one of the movable feasts of the Christian religion. The Nicene Council in A.D. 325 determined that Easter would always fall on the first Sunday after the first full moon on or after March 21st. This meant that Easter would more often than not fall sometime in April.

We cannot overestimate the importance of this feast. Easter celebrates the resurrection of Jesus Christ from the dead. No other event has so changed the course of history. Jesus' resurrection proved that God had accepted the payment Jesus made for the sins of humanity—His own life on the cross. In and through Jesus' dying, we receive forgiveness for our sins. Though we deserve death because of our sins, Jesus died in our place. Because of His resurrection, we will live forever with Him in heaven. "For the wages of sin is death, but the gift of God is eternal life in Christ Jesus our Lord" (Romans 6:23).

———

The Solomon Rosenberg family endured life together in a Nazi death camp. In addition to Solomon and his wife, their two children, Jacob and David, and Solomon's aged parents were imprisoned too.

The first to die in the ovens were the grandparents. They were in their 80s and unable to work the long, grueling hours. Under Nazi policy, since they were unable to "earn" their livelihood in the camp, they forfeited their right to life. Solomon feared the next to go would be David, the youngest, who was slightly crippled. Every morning as the members of the family went their separate ways, Solomon feared it might be the last time he would see David.

Upon returning home one day, his greatest fear had been realized. David was nowhere to be found. He quickly scanned the crowds of people and saw Jacob huddled in a corner crying.

"Where is David? Did they take David today?" he asked.

"Yes," Jacob replied between sobs.

"But where is mother? She was well. She could work. Where is she?"

Jacob looked at his father with tears flowing down his cheeks.

"Papa," he said, "they came for David, and he started to cry. And so Mother pleaded to go along, and they let her. I saw them go, Papa. Mother was holding David in her arms so that he would not be frightened!"[15]

———◦———

During this month we traditionally thank God for His forgiveness through the life, death, and resurrection of

Jesus Christ. It is also a good time to celebrate the forgiveness that the resurrected Christ makes possible in our relationships with others.

On one occasion, one of Jesus' disciples, Peter, asked Jesus, "Lord, how often shall my brother sin against me, and I forgive him? As many as seven times?" (Matthew 18:21 RSV). Jesus' answer shocked the disciples, "I do not say to you seven times, but seventy times seven" (Matthew 18:22 RSV). In other words, forgiveness is to be unlimited. Once you forgive a person "seventy times seven," you won't need rules or limits to the number of times you forgive; forgiveness will be something you will be in the habit of doing.

In the parable of the unmerciful servant (Matthew 18:21–35), Jesus told of a servant who owed 10,000 talents to his master. This was a great deal of money. When the servant begged his master to forgive the debt, the master did just that—solely on the basis of love and mercy. But then the servant went out and demanded payment from a man who owed him a much smaller amount of money. When the man could not pay, the servant had him arrested and thrown into prison. Jesus' point is obvious. As we are forgiven by God through what Christ has done for us, so we should and can go out and share this forgiveness with one another.

The Need to Talk about Forgiveness

We live in a time when few people know much about forgiveness because more and more people are making excuses for their wrongdoing, refusing even to admit that they sin. If they do something wrong, it's blamed on someone else or on the situation. For this reason, Christians, more than ever, need to share and demonstrate God's Word about forgiveness. This includes clarifying what forgiveness is and what it isn't.

Myths about Forgiveness

Myth 1: Forgiveness Is Tolerance of Wrongdoing

Some Christians have gotten too easy on sin—and on sinners. They say things like, "Who am I to judge?" or "God is their judge, not me." Tolerating sin, however, is itself a sin. If we truly care about people and their salvation, we need to care about whether they're living according to God's Word. Jesus Himself would never tolerate wrongdoing. Look at His action at the temple, where "He made a whip out of cords, and drove all from the temple area, both sheep and cattle; He scattered the coins of the money changers and overturned their tables" (John 2:15).

Myth 2: Forgiveness and Forgetting Happen Together

Once forgiveness takes place, forgetting may occur. However, it is wrong to assume that forgiving and forgetting go hand in hand. Forgetting should never be a test of whether a person has forgiven. The miracle of forgiveness is that, with God's help, we can forgive even while we still remember. Paul said, "God demonstrates His own love for us in this: While we were still sinners, Christ died for us" (Romans 5:8).

Myth 3: Forgiveness Is Conditional

Some Christians assume that God's forgiveness depends on whether we forgive others. It doesn't. God's forgiving us is not conditional on what we do or don't do. If it were, we would never be forgiven. He doesn't say, "I'll forgive you as long as you promise never to do it again!" or "I'll forgive you as long as you forgive your brother first." His forgiveness is acceptance—without any exception! The truth is that if we live with bitterness and resentment toward another, if we surround our hearts with an unforgiving spirit, we may also be rejecting God's forgiving mercy.

Myth 4: Forgiveness Is Easy

Forgiveness costs. The forgiveness we received was very costly—it cost Jesus' life. Nor is forgiveness cheap for the Christian. Television and radio evangelists sometimes give the impression that people automatically become loving and forgiving once they become Christians. Such thinking is wrong. To ask for forgiveness, or to grant it, is often very difficult. It's more than just saying, "I'm sorry" or "I forgive you." It means giving up the hatred and resentment that sometimes, sadly, one may even enjoy harboring. It's hard because forgiveness doesn't always fit into the judicial way of thinking; forgiveness doesn't always seem fair.

Scripture gives us many examples of how unfair forgiveness may seem at times. The classic example is the parable of the prodigal son. The prodigal son is welcomed back home despite the fact that he had sinned. He had received what many people felt he deserved—a meal with the pigs. However, when he comes home, his father is "filled with compassion for him … [runs] to his son, [throws] his arms around him and [kisses] him" (Luke 15:20). The older brother tries to reason with his father, in essence asking, "Why? According to my standards, my brother doesn't deserve forgiveness—and he certainly doesn't deserve a party!"

Truths about Forgiveness

Truth 1: Forgiveness Is Made Possible by Jesus

We would not be able to forgive one another had Jesus not earned forgiveness for us. Not only did He earn *our* forgiveness, but He also empowers us to forgive *one another*. He connects us with God so that we can be connected with one another. It happens through Baptism:

> *Don't you know that all of us who were baptized into Christ Jesus were baptized into His death? We were therefore buried with Him through baptism into death in order that, just as Christ was raised from the dead through the glory of the Father, we too may live a new life." (Romans 6:3–4)*

We are also empowered to forgive others through God's Word. Jesus said, "The words I have spoken to you are spirit and they are life" (John 6:63).

Truth 2: Forgiveness Includes Actions

Jesus did more than pronounce forgiveness on His people. He actually *won* forgiveness by going to the cross.

Eliza Doolittle in *My Fair Lady* shouted, "Words, words, I'm tired of words. If you love me, show me!" It's not unusual for a spouse to say, "I'm tired of your promises. If you love me, show me!" Jesus made it clear that forgiveness is not something to be done privately in our closets. It means taking steps toward reconciliation:

> *"Therefore, if you are offering your gift at the altar and there remember that your brother has something against you, leave your gift there in front of the altar. First go and be reconciled to your brother; then come and offer your gift." (Matthew 5:23–24)*

Forgiveness is accompanied by actions.

Truth 3: Forgiveness Is a Present Event

People often suggest that forgiveness is a process, something that happens over a long period of time. "Time heals all wounds." While it's true that time can sometimes help, too often lapsed time makes for more resentment and bitterness, making forgiveness even harder.

Our example of how we should forgive comes from Jesus Christ. Just as we don't have to wait for God to decide if He's going to forgive us, so we should not delay in forgiving someone else. For the Christian, forgiveness is a *lifestyle*. It is something that is here and now—not for tomorrow, but for today. When we find it hard to forgive here and now, it is then more than ever that we need to return to the Word of God and recall His here-and-now forgiveness for us. The Word is a means of grace, a means through which God channels His power to us!

Truth 4: Forgiveness Is Freedom

Christ reminds us: "I tell you the truth, everyone who sins is a slave to sin. ... So if the Son sets you free, you will be free indeed" (John 8:34, 36). Is there anything more freeing than to hear God say to you, "Your sins are forgiven"?

Just as it is freeing to be forgiven, so one is never as free as when one forgives! Corrie ten Boom had been imprisoned for years, along with her sister Betsie, in Nazi concentration camps. Once released, she wrote and lectured on her experiences. At one such lecture in 1947, she was speaking at a Munich church about forgiveness. When the meeting was over, she was shocked to come face to face with a former concentration camp guard, a man she recognized as one of her captors. Since their original meeting, he had become a Christian. Although he knew that God had forgiven him for the cruel things he'd done, he wanted to hear it from her lips—he asked her to forgive him. Here, she recounts that unforgettable meeting and the healing power of forgiveness.

It could not have been many seconds that he stood there, hand held out, but to me it seemed hours as I wrestled with the most difficult thing I had ever had to do.

For I had to do it. ... I knew it not only as a commandment of God, but as a daily experience. Since the end of the war I had had a home in Holland for

victims of Nazi brutality. Those who were able to for-
give their former enemies were able also to return to
the outside world and rebuild their lives. ... Those
who nursed bitterness remained invalids. It was as
simple and as horrible as that.

And still I stood there with the coldness clutch-
ing my heart. But forgiveness is not an emotion. ...
Forgiveness is an act of the will. ... "Jesus, help me!"
I prayed silently. "I can lift my hand. ... You supply
the feeling."

And so woodenly, mechanically, I thrust my
hand into the one stretched out to me. And as I did,
an incredible thing took place. The current started in
my shoulder, raced down my arm, sprang into our
joined hands. And then this healing warmth seemed
to flood my whole being, bringing tears to my eyes.

"I forgive you, brother!" I cried. "With all my
heart!"

For a long moment we grasped each other's
hands, the former guard and the former prisoner. I
had never known God's love so intensely as I did
then.[16]

The Importance of Forgiveness in Marriage

Confession and forgiveness are also an integral part
of every good marriage. Too many marriages fail because
the spouses expect perfection from each other, which is
impossible because Jesus is the only perfect person who

has ever lived. Paul reminds us, "Get rid of all bitterness, rage and anger ... along with every form of malice. Be kind and compassionate to one another, forgiving each other, just as in Christ God forgave you" (Ephesians 4:31–32). Couples who cannot forgive one another will eventually find that bitterness and anger will hound and eventually destroy them.

The Importance of Forgiveness in Parenting

Effective parenting involves being honest and humble enough to admit your own need for forgiveness. Few things are as damaging in a relationship between parents and children as when the parents are too stubborn and arrogant to ever say, "We were wrong, forgive us." If children never hear an admission of wrongdoing from their parents, it's likely they'll turn out to be just as stubborn and self-righteous.

When parents model confession and forgiveness to their children by asking for forgiveness and forgiving, they teach a valuable theological lesson. Sinfulness is a prerequisite for a relationship with Jesus Christ. Jesus said, "It is not the healthy who need a doctor, but the sick" (Matthew 9:12). Jesus suffered death on the cross for those who sin, for those who aren't always right and who desperately need forgiveness.

Christianity is based on forgiveness. Its very foundation is the forgiveness earned for humanity through the life, death, and resurrection of Jesus Christ. It is about reconciliation and restoration. As reconciled, forgiven people, we are more than forgiven. We are enabled to demonstrate such forgiveness toward others, including our wife and our children. To be forgiven and to be able to forgive truly gives us reason for celebration.

❧ Suggestions for Husbands ❧

Week 1

This week, celebrate the forgiveness you and your wife share because of your faith in Jesus Christ.

➤ Find an old clay pot, vase, or other container that's been cracked. Set it someplace where it will be easily seen. Let it serve as a daily reminder that no one is perfect, including you. Whenever you see it, whisper a prayer of thanks for the forgiveness you and your wife have through your faith in Jesus Christ.

➤ Celebrate God's forgiveness by being the first to forgive and forget something your wife did to you.

➤ Memorize 1 John 2:1–2.

➤ Review Ephesians 5:25. Pray that you might love your wife with such a love, including forgiving her as Christ forgives the church.

➤ Read Psalm 51.

➤ Spend 10 minutes in prayer with your wife, thanking God for the gift of forgiveness.

Week 2

This week, review your forgiveness of others, asking whether that forgiveness matches God's forgiveness of you.

➤ Ask yourself these questions in regard to the way

you forgive your wife: *When I forgive her, am I in the cleansing business or the whitewashing business? When she makes a mistake, do I try to rub it in more than out? Do I usually forgive my wife and forget it without reminding her I'm doing it?*

➤ Memorize Ephesians 4:32. Then ask the Holy Spirit to help you practice what it says concerning your wife.

➤ Release a grudge that you have harbored against your wife.

➤ Apologize for something you've done that has hurt your wife.

➤ Be gentle with your wife today.

➤ Have a long conversation with your wife about when you were first married and how your relationship has evolved over the years. At the end, ask forgiveness for the mistakes you've made. Close by saying the Lord's Prayer together.

➤ Dismiss suspicion.

Week 3

This week, make a concerted effort to do more than speak words of forgiveness. Back up your forgiveness with *actions*.

➤ Study Scripture passages that tell how Jesus used more than words in conveying forgiveness and healing. For example, He blessed with meaningful touch (Matthew 20:29–34; Mark 1:40–42; 10:13–16).

- As we have noted, research shows that meaningful touch blesses people physically. When you ask for forgiveness or offer it to your wife, make an intentional effort to convey how you feel with meaningful touch.

- After your next argument, buy your wife a bouquet of flowers to accompany your apology.

- Demonstrate forgiveness as the father did in Luke 15:20.

- Give your wife a night off to do whatever she wishes while you take care of the kids and do other chores around the house.

Week 4

This week, consider the conflict that can occur in your marriage, remaining mindful of what C. S. Lewis said about love. When asked what the opposite of love is (most of us would say hatred), Lewis said indifference. When a person feels something for another person, be it good or bad, he reacts in a certain way. But though these feelings may be negative, they indicate that there is at least some life left in the marriage. It's when a person flat out doesn't care anymore that he or she becomes indifferent.

What happens emotionally in a person's heart is similar to what can happen to the physical heart of a person. An electrocardiogram may indicate an irregular heartbeat or a heart that's not functioning as it should, but the most dangerous electrocardiogram is one that shows a straight line. When one or both of the partners in a marriage become indifferent and uncaring, death is knocking at their door! Ask yourself these questions:

> *Are there times when I treat my wife as though she doesn't exist?* If so, ask forgiveness from God and from her.

> *Do I know what buttons to press to anger my wife or get even with her?* List some of those buttons, and then ask God to forgive you.

> *When I argue, are my words destructive or constructive?* Think of some of the destructive words you use and ask God to forgive you. Then ask for your wife's forgiveness. Attempt to use constructive words to express your opinions in the future.

> *Do I speak the truth in love (Ephesians 4:15)?* If not, tell that truth to your wife and ask for her forgiveness.

> *Are most of our arguments about "nothing" (trivial matters)?* If so, ask yourself why. Is there a bigger issue that needs discussing but is being avoided?

> *Is there indifference in my attitude toward my wife?* If so, pledge to do something about it before it's too late.

⇝ Suggestions for Fathers ⇜

Week 1

This week, celebrate the forgiveness you and your children share because of your faith in Jesus Christ.

➤ Make a concerted effort to share with your children some of the things for which you have specifically asked God to forgive you and your thankfulness in receiving the forgiveness you asked for.

➤ As a family, memorize Micah 7:19.

➤ Read Luke 15:11–32. Then have a party to celebrate your forgiveness.

➤ Sit down with your children. Ask if you've hurt them in any way this last week. If so, ask for their forgiveness.

➤ Share with your children the meaning of this bumper sticker: "Christians aren't perfect; they're just forgiven."

Week 2

This week, review the forgiveness you share with your children, asking whether it matches God's teaching about forgiveness.

➤ Ask yourself these questions in regard to the way you forgive your children: *When I forgive my children, am I in the cleansing business or the whitewashing business? When my children make a mistake, do I try to rub it in more than out? Do I usually forgive my children and forget it without reminding them I'm doing it?*

➢ Make this your prayer for today: "May I not expect the perfection of my children that belongs alone to You."

➢ Study 1 Corinthians 13:4–8. *Does God's definition of love match my love for my children?* If not, ask for forgiveness and for help in being more loving.

➢ Do you speak the truth in love to your children (Ephesians 4:15)?

➢ Is your forgiveness often conditional, as demonstrated by such statements as these? "I forgive you, but I'd better not catch you doing this again!" or "If you ever do this again, that's it!"

Week 3

This week, make a genuine effort to do more than speak words of forgiveness. Back up your words with actions.

➢ When you ask for forgiveness or offer it to your children, convey how you're feeling with meaningful touch.

➢ Make a conscientious effort to communicate your love not only with words but with touch.

➢ Kiss your children and tell them how important they are in God's eyes—enough for Jesus Christ to die for them.

➤ Spend some special time with your children.

➤ Say your next "I'm sorry" through a letter.

Week 4

This week, examine the conflict that occurs between you and your children. Ask yourself these questions:

➤ *Are there times when I treat my children as though they don't exist?* If so, ask forgiveness from God and from your children.

➤ *When I reprimand my children, are my words destructive or constructive?* Think of some of the destructive words you use and ask God to forgive you. Then ask for your children's forgiveness. Attempt to use constructive words in future discussions.

➤ *Do I sometimes major in minors with my children (trivial matters)?* If so, ask God to help you decipher what's major and what isn't.

➤ *Is there indifference in my attitude toward my children in regard to their activities, studies, etc.?* If so, pledge to do something about it before it's too late.

➤ *Do I give at least three compliments for every criticism I give to my children?* If not, start today. Remember, children will respond to whatever gets them some attention.

CELEBRATE REMEMBERING AND RESPECTING

A salesman came home to find his house in complete disarray. This surprised him because his wife was normally a fastidious housekeeper. "What happened?" he exclaimed to his wife.

"Well, honey," she said, "every day when you come home, you ask me the same question, 'What did you do all day?' Well, today I didn't do it."

———❖———

We take for granted how much our wives do—whether they work outside the home or not. They maintain the house, care for the children, cook and clean, and perform other tasks too numerous to count. Similarly we often take God for granted for the things He does for us. Often the only time we appreciate our blessings is when one of them is suddenly taken away—health, wife, children.

May—A Month of Rememberance

Traditionally, we remember some very important people in the month of May. We remember our mothers and our wives on the second Sunday. On the third Saturday, Armed Forces Day, we remember the men and women in America's military services. On Memorial Day, or Decoration Day, May 30th, we remember those who died in the many wars fought by our country. It is good that we remember these special people in the month of May because when we remember them, we *honor* them.

Tips from a Party Crasher

The Scriptures give a wonderful account of a woman who not only remembered someone but gave Him great respect. The story is recorded in Luke 7:36–50. The scene is the home of a Pharisee named Simon who was giving a dinner party. Jesus was his guest of honor.

Very few things are said about the party until a "woman who had lived a sinful life in that town" slips into the room and makes a spectacle of herself. She breaks a jar open and splashes its contents all over Jesus' feet. It is perfume.

Experts tell us that it was not unusual for people in that day to attend a dinner party without being invited—not to eat but to listen to the conversation taking place between the guests. But while eavesdropping was one thing, making a public spectacle of oneself was quite another. Not only did the woman pour perfume all over Jesus' feet, she also kissed His feet, wept aloud, and dried

His feet with her hair. The smell of perfume was every-where throughout the house.

The woman was obviously repentant of her sinful life. Her tears of remorse elicited Jesus' forgiveness. In His lecture to Simon, who silently questioned why Jesus allowed a sinful woman to touch Him, Jesus said: "There-fore, I tell you, her many sins have been forgiven—for she loved much. But he who has been forgiven little loves lit-tle" (Luke 7:47). The woman's love was evidence of her forgiveness.

The "woman who had lived a sinful life" is really each and every one of us. Jesus does the same thing for us as He did for her—He died to redeem us from sin. In recalling this extravagant love for us, we respond by showing Him great respect and honor.

Remembering

The apostle Paul often took comfort from remember-ing the faith of others. While in prison in Rome, he wrote to his faithful and loyal assistant Timothy: "I have been reminded of your sincere faith, which first lived in your grandmother Lois and in your mother Eunice and, I am persuaded, now lives in you also" (2 Timothy 1:5). Timo-thy was twice blessed. He had a Christian mother, Eunice, as well as a Christian grandmother, Lois.

Those of us who have (or had) God-fearing parents have been truly blessed. Too many parents today are noth-ing more than glorified zookeepers. They produce well-educated children suitable only for public display behind iron bars and glass. They provide their children with physical needs but forget their spiritual needs. They bestow on them the latest fashions, the best education, the newest gadgets, but forget to teach them about the things of God. A parent can provide many things—common sense, good manners, good education—but the parent fails if he does not teach a child the answer to life's ultimate question: What happens to me when I die?

> *Billy Graham tells of addressing a large group of university students. During much of the presentation a few students giggled and taunted him. However, there was complete silence when he told a story of a young college student who had been in a serious car accident. The doctor did not expect her to live. The mother of the injured girl rushed to be at the daughter's bedside. As she held her hand, the daughter spoke, "Mother, you taught me much about life. You taught me about the dangers of smoking. You taught me how to hold my cocktail glass. You taught me how to have safe sex, but you never taught me how to die. Teach me quickly, Mom, because I'm dying."* [17]

Remembering our own God-fearing parents can encourage us to lay the same foundation for our children, to "train a child in the way he should go, [so that] when he is old he will not turn from it" (Proverbs 22:6). These memories, more than encouraging us, can help us to encourage our *children*—but only if we share them.

As we remember our own mother and the mother of our children on Mother's Day, we cannot help but think of the sacrifices these women have so selflessly made. There were times when your mother wanted to buy a new dress for herself, but she sacrificed her own needs to buy you a badly needed pair of shoes. There were times when your mother would have liked to sleep in instead of waking up to get you off to school—but she didn't. She lived—and loved—sacrificially.

In May, we also remember and honor those who gave their lives for our country. We do this on Memorial Day, May 30th. We place flowers and other mementos on their graves. We hold parades and attend programs with special music, readings, and eulogies. Despite the value of such remembrances, many communities in the last decade or so have dropped their activities because of lack of attendance. Forgetting has its consequences. Lewis B. Smedes writes in his book *Caring and Commitment*:

> *Every new generation writes a new chapter. But to write their own chapter, children have to know the chapters that went before theirs. This is why we need to hear about the olden days. We need a beginning for our own stories.*[18]

A wise father will help his children know the chapters that precede the ones they will write, including the sacrifices many made to provide the freedoms they now enjoy. Such a valuable lesson might be highlighted by attending a special Memorial Day service.

Respecting

Respecting or honoring often accompanies remembering. It follows as a response. The word *respect* literally means "to look back." On Mother's Day, Armed Forces Day, and Memorial Day, we "look back"—we look back at the many who have been so valuable in our lives, individually and collectively.

There is no better way to teach the value of respect than by example. It's a known fact that male children learn how to respect or disrespect women from their fathers. A father who shows little respect for his wife in the way he talks to her and treats her will teach his son to do the same. Fathers who abuse produce children who abuse!

Failing to respect one's wife and children can bring devastating results. These results may not be apparent immediately, but eventually they will surface. In a way, a family is like a car. If you misuse it by failing to properly maintain it or by driving it in a harmful way, the car eventually stops running. Many families are harmed greatly, not by major malfunction, but through a series of small deteriorations that a little adjusting and tightening now and then could correct. Failing to respect others, to treat them as we would want to be treated, to see them through God's eyes, causes us to eventually believe that they are not valuable.

One of the longest-running programs on public TV is *Mister Rogers.* One of the reasons for its popularity is that children receive respect and affirmation from the master of ceremonies, Fred Rogers. But even better than receiving respect and affirmation from "Mister Rogers" is to receive the same from your *own* father. Such respect begins by treating your children as you yourself would want to be treated, seeing them as God sees them, valuable and precious!

➤ Suggestions for Husbands ➤

Week 1

There's a Gypsy proverb that says, "You have to dig deep to bury your father." Fathers and mothers have a profound impact on their children. Your own father and mother had a profound influence on you. This week, review with your wife some aspects of your own upbringing as well as hers. *How is your upbringing reflected in your parenting?*

➤ Do you accuse your wife of being just like her parents, or worse yet, her mother? Scripture reminds us that a man can often become like he thinks. Spend some time in prayer asking God to forgive you for such remarks. Ask Him for help in preventing you from doing it again.

➤ Send your wife's parents a special card thanking them for raising such a wonderful woman.

➤ If your parents or your wife's parents have offended you, list the offenses, acknowledge the pain they've caused you and your wife, and then resolve to get rid of that pain by bringing the offenses before the Lord. Ask God to help you forgive and forget, as He does with your sins.

Week 2

Celebrate Mother's Day every day this week by creatively honoring your wife.

➤ Give her a day off to do whatever she wants to do.

➤ When a Nobel Prize winner was interviewed about what he considered important, he said, "Two important things are to have a genuine interest in people and to be kind to them."[19] Today, make a conscientious effort to show genuine interest in your wife, what she's thinking about, what she's feeling, what she's dreaming about.

➤ Present your wife with her favorite musical recording. Then listen to it as you sit together on the couch.

➤ Write your wife a romantic letter. Then send it to her in the mail.

➤ Some say that chocolate helps in the romance department. If that's the case in your household, send your wife a large box of chocolates.

➤ Go to your public library and check out a book of romantic poetry. Bring it home and read some of it aloud to your wife.

➤ Just before you turn out the lights, read selections from the Song of Songs to her.

Week 3

Concentrate on showing your wife great respect.

➤ Find a card that summarizes how valuable your wife is to you and your children. Better yet, buy a card that's blank inside and write something yourself.

➤ See your wife through God's eyes.

➤ Concentrate on showing your wife respect through the tone of your voice.

➤ Concentrate on showing your wife respect through positive attending behavior when you communicate (e.g., eye-to-eye contact, warm and friendly body posture, affirming facial expressions).

➤ Treat your wife as you yourself wish to be treated.

➤ Tell your wife—in front of your children—how valuable she is to you.

Week 4

Examine the following definitions of respect, asking yourself whether the definition describes the respect you show your wife. If it doesn't, resolve to change.

➤ *Respect is to have high or special regard for someone.* Do I tell and show my wife by my words and actions that I have a high regard for her?

➤ *Respect is to honor the rights of others.* Do I give my wife freedom to think and feel a certain way? Do I suggest by my words and actions that she doesn't have a right to think or feel a certain way?

➤ *Respect is to have good manners and common courtesy.* Do I use good manners and common courtesy in the way I talk to and treat my wife?

➤ *Respect is seeing someone with "God's eyes."* Do I see my wife as God sees her, forgiven and always loved?

➤ *Respect is "to look back," to find the person God loves.* Do I look for good in my wife, or am I always criticizing and complaining about her?

❯❯ Suggestions for Fathers ❮❮

Week 1

Share with your children positive remembrances of your childhood.

➤ With some pictures of your past in hand, sit down with your children and talk about your parents. Share some of the important lessons they taught you about honesty, responsibility, courage, respect, kindness, etc.

➤ Do with your children one of the favorite things you remember your father doing with you.

➤ Find a board game similar to the kind you had growing up and play it with your children.

➤ Go to the "family cemetery" and locate markers of your ancestors. Talk to your children about what you know of these ancestors.

➤ Share a story with your children that your father told you.

Week 2

Help your children honor their mother by challenging them to do creatively loving things for her throughout the week.

➤ Help your children plan and make a special dinner for their mother, with candles, etc.

➤ Help your children serve your wife breakfast in bed.

➤ Help your children send your wife a gigantic banner-gram wishing her a happy Mother's Day.

➤ Honor your wife by having a star named after her. This can be done through International Star Registry, 34523 Wilson Road, Ingleside, IL 60041; (708) 546-5533.

➤ Help your kids place a special "I love you, Mom" advertisement in the classified section of your local paper.

Week 3

Concentrate on showing your children respect. Ask yourself these questions:

➤ *Am I showing respect to my children by the tone of my voice.*

➤ *Am I showing my children respect by my nonverbal behavior, my posture, my eye contact, my facial expressions, my body language?*

➤ *Do I operate with double standards, expecting my children to do as I say not as I do?*

➤ *Do I treat my children with the same respect that I treat adults?*

➤ *Do I practice good manners around my children, saying such things as "please" and "thank you" to them?*

Week 4

Just as you examined your respect for your wife by using different definitions of respect, do the same with your children.

➤ *Respect is to have high or special regard for someone.* Do I tell and show my children by my words and actions that I have high regard for them?

➤ *Respect is to honor the rights of others.* Do I give my children the freedom to think and feel a certain way? Do I suggest by my words and actions that they don't have a right to think or feel a certain way?

➤ *Respect is to have good manners and common courtesy.* Do I use good manners and common courtesy in the way I talk to and treat my children?

➤ *Respect is seeing someone with "God's eyes."* Do I see my children as God sees them, precious and valuable?

➤ *Respect is "to look back," to find the person God loves.* Do I look for good in my children, or am I always criticizing and complaining about them?

CELEBRATE COMMITMENT

A young man wrote the following letter to his young lover:

> I love you with all my heart.
> I would cross the burning desert to look into your eyes.
> I would climb the highest mountain to be at your side.
> I would forge the swollen river and swim the mighty ocean for a glimpse of your lovely face.
> P.S. I will be over tonight if it doesn't rain.

———◦———

This romantic note is all too typical of many relationships today. "I'll do anything for you honey, if (or when) …" Though many lovers express their love for one another, they do it with strings attached. These conditions or footnotes to their wedding vows aren't spoken aloud, but they're part of the hidden agenda. "I'll be faithful—as long as she doesn't gain 30 extra pounds!" "I'll love her and

keep her for my wife—as long as I feel in love with her."
One survey indicated that many couples go into their first
marriage seeing it merely as a "trial run," not necessarily
seeing it as "forever."

A "Fatherless" Country

"Commitmentphobia" is sorely apparent in many
homes where children are being raised without the presence of their biological father. Though statistics vary, we
know that 40 to 60 percent of all American children will
live in a broken home before they reach age 18. The consequences of these statistics can be dire.

Except for Russia, no nation lost more men during
World War I than Germany. In 1918, after the war, Germany was referred to as "the fatherless nation." Seeking
intimacy and a sense of belonging, many fatherless German children ended up following a man named Adolph
Hitler.

Some call the United States of America a "fatherless
nation" as well, but not because of war. Rather, it's
because too many men have abandoned their responsibilities. They *father* children, but they don't stay around to *be*
a father. Today, one out of three children is born out of
wedlock. Among African-Americans, it's two out of three.
These kids go through life with little or no emotional or
financial support from their biological fathers.

A Perfect Picture of Commitment

The true essence of commitment is best demonstrated in our heavenly Father's love for His people. He did

not create His people and abandon them once He placed them on the earth. He didn't forsake them even after they had disobeyed Him. Instead, He redeemed them. He won them back to Himself through His only-begotten Son's sacrifice on the cross.

God does not base His love on our loving. He never waits for us to do or not do certain things before He loves us. He never waits for us to come around, to get our act together, before He comes around or extends His love to us.

> *You see, at just the right time, when we were still powerless, Christ died for the ungodly. Very rarely will anyone die for a righteous man, though for a good man someone might possibly dare to die. But God demonstrates His own love for us in this: While we were still sinners, Christ died for us. (Romans 5:6–8)*

"… when we were still powerless. … while we were still sinners, Christ died for us" (Romans 5:6, 8). Before we even said, "Lord, I come to you confessing my sins," He came to us with His love. Jesus died in our place, for our sins, because God's very nature and purpose is love (1 John 4:16). Our love for others, though imperfect to say the least, must always reflect His love for us—forever and with no strings attached.

Commitment Is Sacrificial

It's not unusual for a number of couples to describe their marriage as a "50/50 proposition." When couples operate under such a principle, it's not long before one or both of the partners feels he or she is getting less from the other spouse or doing more than his or her fair share. They complain that the other person isn't holding up his or her part of the bargain.

"I scratched your back last. It's your turn."
"I apologized the last time. It's your turn
this time."
"You owe me."

Marriage is seen almost as a business contract.

Marriage is never a 50/50 proposition. It's a 100 percent giving of oneself to the other person. It means sharing oneself physically, emotionally, and spiritually—sharing as God did when He gave His only-begotten Son to die for us. Jesus set aside His rights and lived and died sacrificially for His people. Paul tells husbands to do the same thing, "Husbands, love your wives, just as Christ loved the church and gave Himself up for her" (Ephesians 5:25). This includes setting aside plans and ambitions at times for the sake of sacrificially loving your wife.

Years ago, studies showed that fathers spent up to two hours each day communicating with their children. Today, studies show that most fathers spend an average of 30 to 60 seconds a day actually communicating with each child. Unbelievable? Not if one considers the treadmill most families seem to be on!

A survey of more than 1,500 children asked, "What do you think makes a happy family?" The majority of the children said, "Doing things together."[20] Doing things together includes taking time to throw the ball or to assemble a model plane. It means having "pretend tea and crumpets" or getting on all fours and giving your daughter a horsy-back ride.

———

After the devastating earthquake in Armenia several years ago, a father desperately sought to find his only child who had been buried alive in a collapsed building along with several other children. Everything he had to dig with had been buried in the rubble of his own fallen building. With only his hands, he started tearing away the debris of the collapsed building that entombed his son and his son's friends. He would not quit despite the fact that one of his few surviving friends said it was a futile and useless effort.

For five hours the father dug and found nothing but refused to quit. For eight hours he dug, his hands bloodied from the shattered glass and roughened concrete, but still he would not quit. He continued digging away! For 10 hours he continued digging and yet found nothing. Then 12 hours later, as he pulled away a large boulder, there, in an almost cave-like vacuum, were his son and his son's friends. The son had been hurt but was very much alive. Upon seeing his father, the son's face lit up. "Daddy, I knew you'd come for me. ... I knew I could trust you, that you'd come to find me." As the father reached for his son, his son insisted that he take the other children first, saying, "Daddy, I'm not worried. Take care of the other children first. I know you'll come back for me."

Commitment Is a Choice

Man chooses to love or not to love. He chooses to make a commitment or not to be committed. When a husband walks out on his wife and says, "We were never meant for each other," he is saying, "I no longer choose to love you." If he says, "I don't feel in love with her anymore!" he's really saying, "I do not choose to love her."

Love is never the problem. Love does not fail (1 Corinthians 13:8), people do. A marriages dies because one or both of the partners choose to let it die. They stop working on the marriage. They become indifferent. Indifference is like a straight line on a cardiogram; it signifies that the heart has stopped beating—there is no life left.

Commitment means choosing to keep the vows made at marriage: to "love her, comfort her, honor her, and keep her in sickness and in health and, forsaking all others, be husband to her as long as you both shall live."

It means to "leave his father and mother and be united to his wife" (Ephesians 5:31). Such commitment is a choice—a choice you make, a choice that requires forsaking other loves, including self-love!

Commitment means choosing to take time to teach your children the values that will bring glory and honor to God. It means choosing to spend time with your children, recognizing that they are only young once. It means grabbing each teachable moment to share an important truth about life and death. It means taking time to pray with your children, to read a story, to play a board game. Fathers *choose* to be involved in their children's lives.

Commitment Is Forever

There's a saying that "divorce is forever." The pain of divorce *is* forever, especially for the children of divorce. In her research, Claire Berman discovered that adults who experienced their parents' separation or divorce during their childhood carried a pain and emptiness that never left them, that "continue[d] to affect many aspects of their adult lives."[21]

In sharp contrast to the pain of divorce, a God-directed commitment to one's wife and family can produce a great sense of fulfillment and purpose for the entire family, especially the children. M. Scott Peck, in his best-selling book *The Road Less Traveled*, says:

> *Commitment is inherent in any genuinely loving relationship. Anyone who is truly concerned for the spiritual growth of another knows, consciously or instinctively, that he or she can significantly foster that growth only through a relationship of constancy. Children cannot grow to psychological maturity in an atmosphere of unpredictability, haunted by the specter of abandonment. Couples cannot resolve in any healthy way the universal issues of marriage—dependency and independency, dominance and submission, freedom and fidelity, for example—without the security of knowing that the act of struggling over these issues will not itself destroy the relationship.*[22]

Certainly, as we review our commitment to our family, we recognize our failure to be everything God is to us. We receive cards from our wife and children on Father's Day that laud us as husbands and/or fathers, sometimes so sentimentally and so idealistically that we are even a bit embarrassed because we know we haven't been everything we should be as a husband or a father. However, in knowing God's commitment, in knowing that His Son died for the sins of the world, including our sins of not being the kind of husband or father we ought to be, we can begin again with a clean slate. We can celebrate being a father and a husband and live for the day when all who believe gather together in heaven with the great family of God, committed for eternity.

❖ Suggestions for Husbands ❖

Week 1

Study with your wife God's definition of commitment.

➤ Study portions of the book of Hosea, especially Hosea 1–3. The theme of the book is God's love for His people, even when the people were unfaithful.

➤ Study Luke 15:11–32. Ask whether you are as committed to one another as the father was to his sons.

➤ Study the events of Holy Week (Matthew 26–28). Note the urgency and the necessity of Jesus' sacrificial death. After studying these events, review Ephesians 5:25.

➤ With pen in hand read Romans 5:6–11. Underline with a single line the words that describe your commitment to God and with two lines the words that describe God's commitment to you. After reviewing these powerful words, offer a prayer of thanks for His love.

➤ Study the following Scripture passages: Ruth 1:16–17; Matthew 28:20; Luke 24:7; John 19:30. In what ways do these verses help you define *commitment?*

Week 2

Sacrificially love your wife.

➤ Do something for your wife that she hates to do (e.g., cleaning the toilets).

➤ Make your point without getting angry.

➤ Write your wife a love letter. Ask her to keep it in her purse to look at whenever she needs encouragement.

➤ Tell your wife "I love you" in front of others.

➤ Draw her a bubble bath.

➤ Call her from work and tell her you miss her.

➤ Set aside something you planned to do and tell your wife that you're at her disposal to do whatever she would like you to do.

➤ Give up watching TV tonight and just talk to your wife.

➤ Women thrive on intimacy derived from sharing feelings. Whenever you talk with her today, listen to what your wife says she's feeling. Then communicate back to her so she feels understood.

➤ Do something nice for your wife but don't tell her you did it.

➤ Forget the Joneses next door.

Week 3

Set aside time to intentionally show your wife how much you love her.

➤ Write a letter to your wife with three paragraphs. The first paragraph should begin with these words: "I love you when … (you listen to my concerns about work without interrupting)." Begin the second paragraph with these words: "I love you because … (you make my life complete)." The third paragraph should begin with these words: "I love you although … (we don't agree on everything)." The third paragraph is the most important. It embraces agape love—love that isn't based on prerequisites, conditions, or boundaries. This love isn't based on the lovability of the other person. It is God-given love. It is committed love.

➤ Tell your wife how much you love her in your own words.

➤ Discuss the word *commitment* with your wife. What does it mean to you? to her?

➤ After your children have overheard an argument between you and your wife, sit down with them and remind them that though you may argue at times, you and their mom are committed to each other forever, just as Jesus is committed to His people.

➤ Leave notes around the house expressing your love for her (e.g., on steamy bathroom mirrors).

Week 4

Let your wife know that commitment is forever.

➤ Ask your pastor for a copy of the wedding vows. After reviewing them with your wife, hold hands and speak the vows to one another.

➤ Ask your wife to describe the picture she sees of your life together when you retire. Then share your ideas with her.

➤ Study John 14:1–6.

➤ Discuss the following slogan with your wife: "More men run away from home than teenagers." In what ways do men run away from home other than physically walking out? How can being a workaholic be a form of running away? If you've removed yourself from your wife, ask for her forgiveness.

➤ Study 1 Corinthians 7:1–5. Question whether you have subconsciously accepted the myth that as one ages, he should no longer be interested in sex or is unable to have sex.

➤ Demonstrate that your home is a "grace place," a place where the Gospel is lived out.

➤ Remember, you can't change others. You can only change yourself with the Holy Spirit's help.

❧ Suggestions for Fathers ☙

Week 1

Study with your children God's definition of commitment.

➤ Study Luke 15:11–32. Remind your children that the father represents not only our heavenly Father but also their earthly father. Hug your children and tell them you'll always love them.

➤ Study Romans 5:6–11. In celebration of what it says, treat your children to ice cream or another favorite treat!

➤ Consider the following statement, "I do not love him because he is good, but because he is my little child." Tell your children the same truth using your own words.

➤ Explain to your children what 1 John 3:1 means to you.

Week 2

Sacrificially love your children.

➤ Discuss with your children the truthfulness of this statement: "I may not like what you do, how you act, or what you think at times, but I will always love you despite what you do, how you act, or what you think at times."

➤ Encourage your children to give 100 percent effort in whatever they do.

➤ Go out of your way to help your children today. After you've done so, tell your children that you hope they'll do the same for someone else.

➤ Love your children enough not to rescue them from the consequences of their actions when those consequences won't seriously harm them.

➤ Though it may be faster for you to do it alone, ask your children to help you with a task you have to do, such as washing your car (or even changing the oil, if you dare!). Encourage your children to do as much of it as possible by themselves.

Week 3

Set aside time to intentionally show your children how much you love them.

➤ Take the day off and go to the zoo or an amusement park with your children.

➤ Do today what you've been promising to do for your children for weeks.

➤ Love your children with words of praise.

➤ Give your children snapshots of their strengths (e.g., "I love the way you help your sister" or "You are really a big help to Mom when you set the table").

➤ Place a self-stick note on the mirror of your children's bathroom with a special message from you.

➤ If appropriate, take time today to teach your children an important truth about sex or having children from

God's Word (e.g., Genesis 1:26–28; 2:24; Deuterono-my 24:5; Psalm 127:3–5; Proverbs 5:18–20; Song of Songs 4:1–7; 5:3; 5:9–16; 6:13–7:9; 7:10–13; 8:6; Malachi 4:6; 1 Corinthians 7:3–5; Hebrews 13:4).

➤ Support your wife's disciplinary actions.

➤ Love your children enough to discipline them.

Week 4

Teach your children that commitment is forever.

➤ Chuck Swindoll, in his book *Come Before Winter and Share My Hope*, writes of his dad's death:

> *My dad died last night. ... As I stroked the hair from his forehead and kissed him good-bye, a hundred boyhood memories played around in my head. ... From him I learned to seine for shrimp. How to gig flounder and catch trout and red fish. How to open oyster shells and fix crab gumbo ... and chili ... and popcorn ... and make rafts out of old inner tubes and gunny sacks. ... The memories are as fresh as this morning's sunrise.*[23]

Consider the same scene with a different cast of characters. You are the father who has died. Your son or daughter is reminiscing as he or she strokes your hair from your forehead and kisses you good-bye. What memories will he or she be recalling? What are you hoping he or she will remember?

➤ Review Romans 8:35–39.

➤ Give your children a Bible. As you do, remind them of the words in 1 Peter 1:24–25.

➤ Make sure your children know the answer to life's ultimate question: What happens to me when I die? (The answer is found in John 3:16.)

➤ Let your children know that you will always love them.

CELEBRATE RESPONSIBILITY

In today's America, everyone seems to be talking about rights: "I have a right to do what I want with my body!" and "You know we have our rights!" Advocacy groups espouse the rights of children. Lawyers trumpet the rights of their clients, "Just call 1-800-SUE-THEM, and I'll get you what you deserve, even if the accident *was* your fault." An article in *Time* magazine said we have become a society full of crybabies, finger-pointers, and eternal victims. Though we hear lots of talk about rights, we hear very little about responsibilities or obligations. Winston Churchill said, "The price of greatness is responsibility." Alexander Solzhenitsyn said in a commencement speech to the students of Harvard, "It is time to promote human responsibility."

A Perfect Picture of Responsibility

There is no better picture of someone giving up His rights than Jesus Christ:

Who, being in very nature God, did not consider equality with God something to be grasped, but made Himself nothing, taking the very nature of a servant, being made in human likeness. And being found in appearance as a man, He humbled Himself and became obedient to death—even death on a cross! (Philippians 2:6–8)

Jesus Christ actually laid aside the use of His rights as God when He took manhood upon Himself, all because of His great love for people. Nothing was more degrading than crucifixion, but neither was anything more needed by the world than forgiveness, release from the power of the devil, and eternal life. Such was the responsibility Jesus was willing to take upon Himself for the sake of His people. Paul writes, "Your attitude should be the same as that of Christ Jesus" (Philippians 2:5).

In a world that seems to be so irresponsible, it's imperative that parents teach their children how to be responsible, even if it means giving up some of their rights. In his book *Parents Passing On the Faith,* Carl Spackman defines the purpose of parenting as "to de-parent," to train one's children with ample life skills so that the children might be set free to live God-pleasing, responsible lives, without depending on their parents.[24]

Accepting Consequences

We teach our children responsibility when we help them see and experience the impact of the choices they make. Parents sometimes excuse the misbehavior of their children, blaming it on the circumstances, the teacher at preschool, or some other scapegoat. This only blinds the children to the real cause of their misbehavior and actually makes them morally irresponsible.

Though there may be a myriad of reasons why parents bail their children out of trouble, some parents do it because it's a way of handling their own guilt for not investing personally in their children's lives. When children always get bailed out, they learn to believe that even when they make bad decisions, someone will be there to undo the consequences. Even worse, they'll often keep misbehaving because it's the only way they can continue to get the attention they crave from their fathers!

Solomon helps us see how today's actions can affect tomorrow's realities. In his illustration of the ants preparing for winter, he wrote: "Go to the ant, you sluggard; consider its ways and be wise! It has no commander, no overseer or ruler, yet it stores its provisions in summer and gathers its food at harvest" (Proverbs 6:6–8). What we as human beings fail to do at times, the ant does instinctively. The consequences of not storing up food are obvious. What we sow, we shall also reap (Galatians 6:7–9). If children aren't taught to take responsibility for their choices and suffer the resulting consequences, it will be hard for them to change any harmful patterns that emerge.

Dreaming Dreams

We teach our children to be responsible when we help them dream dreams and guide and direct them to fulfill those dreams. As discerning parents, we must not determine these dreams on the basis of what we ourselves may want our children to become. For example, a father may have always dreamed about being a great football player but never quite made it, so he transfers his dream to his son. Any dream must be determined on the basis of the child's likes and dislikes, her abilities and gifts, never on a parent's unfulfilled dreams. Children need to have an area of competence. This can give them a sense of meaning and accomplishment.

Helping children be responsible begins early, perhaps with something as simple as giving them the responsibility of feeding the parakeet every morning. It means affirming them and letting them know they did a good job. It includes lovingly guiding your children when they haven't fulfilled their obligations. It means encouraging and helping them use their gifts and abilities to the fullest. It means acknowledging and recognizing imperfections, improving those that are correctable, and compensating for those that aren't.

The dreams we help our children dream must be of things that truly matter in God's eyes, such as kindness, gentleness, and a forgiving heart. They must include what is most important—an eternal future with Jesus Himself.

Living the Truth

We teach responsibility, too, when we speak and live the truth and teach our children to do the same. If you instruct your child to tell the person who has just asked to talk to you on the telephone that you're not there even though you are, you are teaching him a dangerous pattern.

We need to be sure that we don't teach our children that success comes from conniving or manipulating people or rules (especially God's rules). A child's behavior will be consistent with what he or she believes to be true. The truth helps children face the realities of life. They are then able to deal with the bad things and enjoy the good things.

Selecting Proper Heroes

We need to ask our children who their heroes are and what these heroes represent to them. What are these heroes' lifestyles saying or not saying to our children? For example, a few years ago a famous athlete announced that he was infected with HIV, the AIDS-related virus. Unfortunately, he did not say, "I sinned. I was promiscuous!" Instead he said something similar to this, "Before I was married, I truly lived the bachelor's life. … I did my best to accommodate as many women as I could … most of them through unprotected sex." We as fathers, in our zeal and love for sports, may fail at times to call our children's attention to the unchristian behavior of some of these heroes, thereby sending dangerous signals to our children, especially when our children see us cheering these heroes on.

Imitating Parents

A cartoon shows a young woman throwing up her hands in disgust as she tries to beat the tax deadline. "Why do I always wait till the last minute?" she exclaims. She looks at her parents, who are standing to her side. "I know why," she says. "Because *you* always waited until the end." She continues to sort through boxes of loose papers and asks, "Why do I keep all my papers stuffed in one box?" Looking at her parents, she exclaims once again, "Because that's exactly what I saw *you* do all your life." In the last frame you see the father looking at the mother and asking, "Do we rejoice or weep that she followed in our footsteps?" Children will imitate parents.

A father who wants to teach his children how to treat their future spouses begins by treating his own wife in a loving, kind, and considerate way. A man who threatens a divorce every time something goes wrong is flashing harmful pictures before his children. He's saying that when there's failure or disappointment, one is no longer obligated to his or her promises. A solid foundation of love and commitment between a husband and wife will teach invaluable lessons to their children.

Sacrificially Loving Wives

Husbands are told to "love [their] wives, just as Christ loved the church and gave Himself up for her" (Ephesians 5:25). Paul sets for husbands a very high standard—the standard of Christ Himself, who loved the church enough to give His life for it. "God made Him who had no sin to be sin for us, so that in Him we might become the righteousness of God" (2 Corinthians 5:21). We love our wives when we are as Christ was to the church—sacrificial in our loving. It might mean giving up "Monday Night Football" (or at least the first half!) to help her bathe the children. It might mean asking yourself some real soul-searching questions about the words you speak to your wife—"Are they words I would like to have spoken to me by someone who says she loves me?" It means treating your wife as the most precious thing in your life. It means saving the best hours and the best effort for her, not the TV or the golf course.

Certainly one of the themes we celebrate in our observance of the Fourth of July is that of responsibility. What if George Washington hadn't taken responsibility for the conduct of the Revolutionary War? We might not even have an Independence Day today. There are ways in which husbands and fathers can be more responsible in loving their wives and children.

➤ Suggestions for Husbands ⥺

Week 1

This week, celebrate both independence and dependence—the independence of your country and the dependence you and your wife have on each other. Upon creating man, God saw that man was lonely. He needed a "helpmate." Celebrate your partnership with your wife, her insight and discernment, her counsel and love. Let her know you depend on her. Prepare for this week's activities by reading 1 Corinthians 13:1–13.

➤ Do something special this evening with your wife. It doesn't have to be expensive. It might simply be having a cup of coffee at a local restaurant. Share with her why she's so important to you.

➤ Bring home a special gift for your wife—a flower, a box of candy, a new negligee.

➤ Someone once said, "Women are like gigantic sponges. You can fill them up each day with compliments, but by the next morning they've been squeezed out and you need to start all over." Today, make every effort to compliment your wife for as many things as you can.

➤ Hug your wife tightly and say, "I love you."

➤ Tell your wife why you think she's the greatest mom in the world.

> Do the dishes tonight.

> Write special love-notes and hide them in places she'll discover tomorrow.

Week 2

Meditate on Christ's love and try as much as possible to imitate that love. Prepare for this week's activities by reading Ephesians 5:23–33.

> Sharing feelings is a high priority for most women. Share today how you feel about your wife.

> Think about this saying: "An attractive woman is made, not born."

> Treat your wife as your best friend.

> Recall some of the humorous times in your marriage. Share some of the funny details and then laugh together.

> Give up one of your favorite TV programs and invite your wife to sit down and talk with you. Let her choose the subject.

> Take a walk together. Hold each other's hand.

> Kowtow to your wife's wishes.

> Identify your contributions to any problems the two of you are having and apologize for them.

> There are many languages of love. Some include a kind act, a kind word, a gift, and time. Share one of each with your wife today.

Week 3

A husband who loves his wife takes responsibility for his actions. He doesn't get caught up in the Adam-Eve syndrome of blaming or excusing. Review Psalm 51 as preparation for this week's activities.

➤ Apologize to your wife for something you did wrong. Ask for her forgiveness.

➤ Talk to your wife about something that has bothered you for some time. Then release the grudge.

➤ Reflect on the way it was when you dated each other—how you used to sit on the couch, hug, and hold hands. Repent for the things you have done that have diminished the excitement you once experienced in your marriage. Then do what you once did.

➤ Ask your wife, "What one thing do I do that really bothers you?" Once she's told you, don't argue. Pray, asking God to help you change and not do what is bothersome to her.

➤ Do one special thing today to show your wife how important she is.

➤ Spend some time with your children.

Week 4

A husband who loves his wife shares dreams with her—dreams of what he wants in life and dreams of things they share as a couple. Prepare for this week's activities by reading Jeremiah 29:11.

➤ Take a walk together. As you walk, have each complete this statement: "Ten years from now, I hope to ..."

➤ Remember your wedding day by looking through your wedding pictures or watching your wedding video. Who was your best man? What's happened to him? In what ways have you changed physically? What dreams did you have then? Which dreams have you fulfilled? Which do you still dream?

➤ Ask your wife what kind of future she pictures for your children. Compare her picture with the one you have for them.

➤ Write a special love note to your wife using words that will help mold and shape her into reaching her potential.

➤ Assure your wife today that nothing but death will part you.

➤ Share with your wife what you hope your children will remember most about you some day. Ask your wife to share what she hopes the children will remember about her.

⤜ Suggestions for Fathers ⤛

Week 1

During the first week and in keeping with a July theme, help your children reflect on their civic responsibility. Help them see that they are not islands unto themselves. They have God-given responsibilities to their country. As you prepare for this week, consider Romans 13:1–10.

➤ Take your children through a local cemetery. Identify the grave sites of those who gave their lives for their country. Talk to your kids about their responsibility for the preservation of freedom.

➤ Plant a tree with your child. Ask your child to be the tree's special friend or caretaker.

➤ Help your child write a letter to the president of the United States. Encourage your child to ask a question or to make a comment. Make the letter short. The address is The White House, 1600 Pennsylvania Avenue, Washington, D.C. 20500.

➤ Bake a "Happy Birthday, U.S.A." cake with your children. (Warning: If you've never baked a cake before, it might be wise to ask your wife to leave the house for a few hours!) Decorate the cake with candles. At dinner, sing "Happy Birthday, U.S.A." and blow the candles out. Add ambiance by drinking red fruit punch with blue ice cubes.

➤ Decorate your bikes or tricycles with red, white, and blue streamers. Take a ride through the neighborhood.

➤ Go to a local park. Bring two trash bags, one for you and one for your child. See who can collect the most trash. (Wearing gloves is always a good idea.)

➤ Read a book about patriotism together.

Week 2

Teach your children something about financial responsibility. Our money and possessions are gifts from God. He requires us to be wise and faithful stewards of all we have. Study Matthew 25:14–30 as preparation for this week.

➤ Talk to your child about credit cards. Explain how they work and the responsibility you have when you acquire one.

➤ Help someone in need. Take your children along. Let them help too. Help your children see that helping someone in need is more than a responsibility, it is a privilege. In sharing, you are thanking God.

➤ Americans save less than five percent of their income. If you haven't already, help your child set up a savings account. Review Proverbs 6:6–8 together.

➤ Teach your children the principle of tithing. Get them offering envelopes. Ask them to designate one envelope for each Sunday and to place for the next Sunday's offering a certain percentage of their allowance or money earned into the envelope immediately upon receiving it.

➤ Ask your children to join you in cleaning out their closet. (You might want to get mother's help in doing this.) Then together, take the clothing they no longer wear to the local Salvation Army outlet or a thrift shop. Too often, this has been something mothers have done. Fathers make a big impression when they participate in delivering these items to the needy.

➤ Purchase a special piggy bank and label it "Daddy-Son/Daughter Fun Fund." Put all your loose change in the bank. Choose one day each month to go out and use the money you've saved to have some fun. Go even if the bank's light.

➤ Ask your kids if you can help them with their chores. After you've helped, thank them for the privilege.

Week 3

Help your children reflect on being morally responsible. In an age of excusing and accusing, we need to help our children recognize their moral and ethical responsibilities. As you prepare for this week consider James 1:13–15.

➤ Review God's Ten Commandments (Exodus 20:3–17). Remind your children that these are more than God's suggestions, they are God's *commandments*.

➤ Proclaim today No-Excuses Day. Make a game of seeing how long each member of the family can last without making some excuse for why he or she did or didn't do something (e.g., "I couldn't make my bed because I overslept").

> Buy the age-appropriate book and video for your child from the Learning about Sex series (Concordia Publishing House). Use this series to help teach your child his or her moral responsibilities in the area of sexuality.

> Discuss the words *sin* and *repentance* with your child. Give a personal example of some sin you've committed this last week. Share your sorrow over the sin. Explain how repentance actually offers hope and freedom. We don't have to think up excuses anymore. We stand forgiven through Jesus Christ.

> Review together your family's TV viewing. What are your favorite programs? Do these programs reinforce the values and morals you wish for your children?

> Spend some extra time today with your heavenly Father, asking for guidance and direction in raising your child to be morally responsible.

> Tell your child today what kind of spouse you hope he or she will someday choose.

Week 4

Help your children reflect on being responsible in their relationships with God and others. Too many relationships are built on lies. One survey shows that 91 percent of Americans admit to lying routinely. Pride often gets in the way in our relationship with

God and others. For any of us to truly know intimacy in any relationship, it must begin with honesty. As you prepare for this week, consider 1 John 1:8–10.

➤ Read a book on manners, such as *The Family Book of Manners* by Hermine Hartley (Barbour & Co., 1990). Well-mannered people are much more apt to be self-assured and capable of coping in a variety of social settings.

➤ Ask your children to join you on a walk. During the walk, talk about honesty and how much you want them to be honest with you about everything. Tell them that even though you may disagree with what they're doing or have done, you'll always love them.

➤ Write a long-overdue letter to some family friends. Ask your children to write a portion of the letter.

➤ Ask your children to tell you what they did today. You do nothing but listen!

➤ Apologize to your child for something you did wrong. Ask your child to forgive you.

➤ Take your child out for a soda and a talk.

➤ Plant a big kiss on your child before you leave for work.

CELEBRATE TIME TOGETHER

"Summertime and the livin' is easy," wrote Ira Gershwin. August marks the height of summer. Though it's usually one of the hottest months, August finds our nation's highways, railways, and airways jammed with people trying to get away from the crowds. August means vacation—a time for "fishin' " and "livin' easy."

The real problem with vacations for many people is that their vacations become more tiring than work itself. You hurry to get away only to find that the rest of the world seems to have gotten there before you did. You seek respite and relaxation only to find that the same old family quarrels and arguments accompany you. Could it be that vacations often fail to really be vacations because we have the wrong expectations? Could it be that we prepare in every other way—the proper cooking utensils, the firewood, the camp site, the food, the flashlights—but forget to bring along what's most important, that which promises to bring *real* rest—God's Word (Matthew 11:28–29)?

Some Vacation Tips from God

Jesus knew pressures. He knew what it was like to "have to get away."

> *Then, because so many people were coming and going that they did not even have a chance to eat, He said to [the apostles], "Come with Me by yourselves to a quiet place and get some rest." (Mark 6:31)*

Jesus had to get away from time to time. And when He did, He took advantage of the resources available to Him. In one of His most difficult hours, just before His crucifixion, He retreated into the Garden of Gethsemane for one reason—to pray. After communing with God in intimate prayer, He told His disciples, "Rise, let us go! Here comes my betrayer" (Matthew 26:46). His retreat, His time at Gethsemane, helped Him to journey forward. Every time He retreated, Jesus came back with a clear perspective of His purpose and the work that was required to accomplish that purpose.

Many of us consider a vacation a chance to "get away from it all." And while we certainly need to do that at times, a vacation should be more than waiting in lines at Disneyland or traveling 2,000 miles to visit relatives. It should restore us physically, emotionally, and spiritually. It should help us see things more clearly, get a better perspective. It might be compared to a person looking at a great oil painting. To fully appreciate its beauty, one must stand some distance away from the painting. If you stand too close, all the colors seem to spill together. In like manner, a vacation should help us focus on the things that are really important.

Just as Jesus took advantage of the resources available to Him, so we must take advantage of the resources He provides for us—Word and Sacrament. We know that the Word has great power because we have seen what it has done in our lives, yet when we need it the most, we often neglect it. We leave on vacation and remember everything but the Bible. Too many people vacation not only from the grind of everyday chores but also from Sunday-morning worship. We recharge all the other batteries—physical and emotional—but forget to recharge our spiritual batteries. Jesus makes it clear what's most important: "But seek first His kingdom and His righteousness, *and all these things will be given to you as well*" (Matthew 6:33, emphasis added).

Make the Most of Your Vacation

There are other things we can do to make our vacations more enjoyable.

- *Don't have unrealistic expectations of one another.* When traveling, I want to conquer the 500-mile journey in one fell swoop. My wife, on the other hand, likes to stop along the way to shop, sightsee, even picnic. It is wise to discuss the differences you have in traveling before you start on the trip. Come up with a compromise where everyone feels as if they're winners.

- *Make your vacation a family event by involving everyone in its planning and preparation.* Make sure the youngest to the oldest feels like they are a part of it. Assign one to read the road map. Another might plan the games to play while in the car. Another could check out the hotel.

- *Don't come home from your vacation more exhausted than you were before you left.* Schedule enough time to do the things you really want to do. Few things are more harried than a vacation that turns out to be nothing more than running here and there and not really doing what you want or need to do—relax. Remember, vacation is a special time for you and your wife, a time to spend some quality moments together, even if it's after the kids go to bed. It's a time for you and your wife—and your children—to reconnect!

- *Pledge to be nice to each other during the trip.*

- *Don't let your vacation make you feel good enough to return to work and so poor you have to.* In other words, don't overspend your budget. You'll be sorry later.

- *Create memories.*

- *Do something you've never done before as a family.* There's nothing as bad as making your vacation seem like the way you view your work sometimes—boring. This happens when you don't stretch your imagination, when you refuse to be spontaneous, when you get into a rut year after year!

- *Carefully record the highlights of your vacation.* Videotape them. One member of the family might collect mementos. Another might keep a journal.

Take Mini-Vacations

Not every vacation has to be an extravagant once-in-a-lifetime affair. In fact, some families insist that their best vacations have been when they've just stayed at home and done the local stuff! They go to the park and play ball. They read up on local history and discover local landmarks. They camp in their backyard.

A vacation should build relationships. It should be a time when you and your wife review the things that have happened over the last year. It should be a time to dream about what you'd like to see in the future. It should be a time when you and your children get better acquainted. It should be a time when you encourage one another and play together with great abandon. It should be a time when you laugh together.

Vacation from TV

The average American family watches more than 50 hours of TV per week. For many families, TV is like the Trojan horse; we allow it into our home, and then it takes over. We have put TVs in our living rooms, bedrooms, kitchens, even our camping trailers, and we allow them to dictate to our families what's right and wrong, spewing out values contrary to what we believe. Every time we turn on the TV, we are inviting someone in to sell us something. The only communication that takes place is one way—directly from the producers and directors of the programming and commercials to the viewers.

The average American 16-year-old has seen more

than 200,000 acts of violence and 33,000 murders on TV. Research has found a definite connection between what children see on TV and the violence seen in our nation's streets, communities, and homes. One study shows that as many as one-third of all violent crimes committed by children are reenactments of events they had earlier witnessed on TV.

Violence is but one byproduct of bad TV. More and more shows are showcasing sex—more than 90 percent of which involves unmarried couples. From the afternoon soaps to talk shows, the subject is sex (and invariably, it's the wrong kind of sex). The National Family Foundation reports that 72 percent of junior-high boys and 44 percent of junior-high girls want to imitate what they see in sexually oriented movies.

Michael Medved, in his best-selling book *Hollywood vs. America*, says there's a war going on between America and Hollywood. He suggests that the entertainment business follows its own dark obsessions rather than what the public wants, that the industry has attacked families, glorified brutality, and demeaned religion. He urges responsible people to demand that Hollywood be more accountable for what it brings to us via TV and the big screen.

During vacation, while the family is all together, establish a policy regarding TV, especially since the beginning of school is right around the corner. Here are a few suggestions.

- Determine how many hours of TV each child may watch per day.

- Determine what type of shows may be watched.

- Keep your children from developing a love affair with their TVs by not allowing a set in their bedroom.

- Don't use the TV as an electronic baby-sitter.

- Replace broadcast or cable TV with your own in-home video library.

- Pray for those Christians who are working inside the entertainment industry, that the Holy Spirit might use them to make a difference.

- Give your children a standard by which they can make sound judgments on what they watch and listen to.

- Make sure your baby-sitter knows the rules in your house regarding TV viewing.

- Pray that God would give each member of your family a discerning spirit regarding what to watch and not watch.

August is a good time to prove to yourself that you can do without TV or at least limit your viewing drastically. It's a good time to take a real vacation—a vacation from TV. Instead of your family sitting in front of the old boob tube, sit on the front porch and talk or play a board game.

10 Things TV Can't Do

1. TV can't hold your child in its lap and read to him.

2. TV can't hug your child.

3. TV can't put a thermometer into your child's mouth.

4. TV can't provide one-on-one communication with your child.

5. TV can't put a baseball into your child's glove.

6. TV can't call your child by name.

7. TV can't smell like Daddy's cologne.

8. TV can't empathize with your child when she cries.

9. TV can't kiss your child's cheek and say good night.

10. TV can't provide a listening ear.

Someone defined a vacation as "a brief period of recreation, preceded by a period of anticipation, and followed by a period of recuperation." But it doesn't have to be that way if you plan your vacation carefully. With the right planning, a vacation can be a celebration of who you are (and to whom you belong). It can be a time when everyone's spirits soar and are restored.

➤ Suggestions for Husbands ➤

Week 1

Discuss your vacations—past, present, and future.

➤ Discuss with your wife your expectations of a vacation.

➤ Talk about memorable vacations you've each experienced. What made them memorable?

➤ Take a mini-vacation this week (e.g., check into a nearby hotel and pretend you're far away from home).

➤ Review some of the highlights of previous vacations by looking at pictures, videos, or postcards.

➤ Start planning next year's vacation.

➤ Buy a travel book about a place you'd like to visit (like the Caribbean). Study it and dream a little.

Week 2

Review your TV viewing.

➤ Discuss with your wife how many hours of TV you feel your family should watch each day.

➤ Go through the *TV Guide* and mark the programs you think are appropriate and inappropriate for your family.

➤ Pray for those Christians working inside the entertainment industry, that the Holy Spirit might use them to make a difference.

> Write out rules for TV viewing in your house. Post them on the refrigerator for everyone to see, including the baby-sitter.

> Pray that each member of your family might have a discerning spirit regarding what to watch on TV.

Week 3

Take a vacation from TV. Instead of watching it do the following:

> Take a hike and smell the flowers along the way. Really smell them. Get on your knees and stick your nose right into them.

> Play a game with your children.

> Read the book of Ruth.

> Enjoy the fellowship of your neighbors around the picnic table.

> Play a game of Pictionary or Balderdash.

> Take turns reading a book aloud.

> Delight in the warm summer evening. Sit on the porch and listen to the sound of katydids.

> Go to a romantic place and watch the sun set.

Week 4

Do some of these things while you're on vacation (or the next time you go on vacation).

➤ Smile a lot.

➤ Do something nice for someone you don't know.

➤ Stop and visit a church along the way, even if it's not Sunday.

➤ Keep a daily journal.

➤ Play a game. Be a good loser. Be a good winner!

➤ Invite the family to lie on their backs and look at the stars.

➤ Take lots of pictures.

⋙ Suggestions for Fathers ⋘

Week 1

Discuss with your children past, present, and future vacations.

> Review your last vacation. Ask your children what they liked and didn't like about it. Look at the pictures or videos you took.

> Dream about future vacations. Ask each child, *If you could choose a vacation to anywhere, where would you want to go?*

> Take a mini-vacation this weekend—to the beach, camping, fishing—anything that gets you away from the "maddening crowds."

> Think of someone who never gets to go on vacation. Why not make plans to take him or her along with you on your next one?

> Write down all the things you hope will happen when you go on your next vacation (e.g., relax, read a favorite book).

> Play "Pretend You're on the Perfect Vacation." What will it look like it? How will it make you feel?

Week 2

Discuss your family's TV viewing habits.

> Discuss with your children what you think is a fair

amount of time for each member of the family to watch TV each day.

➤ Review with your children programs you feel are appropriate for the family to watch. Use your *TV Guide* or some other source that lists area programming.

➤ Discuss with your children what they think are appropriate rules for watching TV in your home. Write down the agreed-upon rules and post them on the refrigerator for everyone to see.

➤ Review James 1:14–15. How might James' words describe a person who continually watches harmful TV programming? Ask your children which programs they believe are harmful and why.

➤ Discuss this statement: "Every time we turn on the TV, we're inviting someone in to sell us something."

Week 3

Take a vacation from TV. Instead of watching it do the following:

➤ Play tag football in the backyard.

➤ Sit in your backyard and talk.

➤ Read a story to your child.

➤ Show your child how to change the oil in the car.

➤ Go swimming.

➤ Buy a quart of your children's favorite ice cream and go to the park to eat it.

- Put together a huge 500-piece puzzle on your coffee table.

- Plan a backyard circus. Invite grandparents and neighbors. Each member of the family has to be part of the circus—a clown, someone who does card tricks, leader of a pet parade, etc.

- Make a summer memory book.

- Teach your children that sharpening their skill at a sport is better than watching that sport on TV. Invite them to practice the sport with you.

Week 4

Do some of these things while you're on vacation (or the next time you go on vacation).

- Show respect for everything and everybody!

- Instead of "whistle while you work," whistle while you take a family hike.

- Remind everyone in the car that they're your most precious cargo, so buckle up!

- When someone tells you something exciting about what they saw or experienced, just listen. Don't try to top their story.

- Learn five clean jokes. Teach them to your children. As you do, laugh a lot.

- Say hello to a stranger.

- Make chili with your children while Mom relaxes.

➤ Live as though today were your last day with your children.

➤ Live today in such a way that your epitaph could read, "With No Regrets."

➤ Take a nap with your children under the sun.

CELEBRATE WORKING AND LEARNING TOGETHER

The old *Ed Sullivan Show* offered a variety of colorful acts. One in particular was featured often—and always to the audience's delight. A man would walk out on stage with a pile of ceramic plates, place them on a table, and then start spinning one plate at a time on three-foot sticks. He'd keep moving down the table, putting more and more plates on sticks, until they were all spinning away.

Toward the end of the table, the plate spinning on the first stick would start to wobble and run out of steam. The man would run to it, give it another spin, and then do the same to the next plate, which also had started to falter. Up and down the line he would go, keeping half a dozen plates or more whirling. Finally, perhaps out of sheer exhaustion, he would let each plate fall into his hands until every one was back where it had started—in the stack.

When a man gets married, he might be compared with the man spinning his first plate. Before long, more and more plates are added—increased work load, the purchase of a home, the first child—and the first plate, his marriage, begins to wobble because of neglect. Quite often, work seems to capture more of his attention than any of the other spinning plates, including his marriage. The results can be tragic.

An Examination of Your Labor

The only legal public holiday in September is Labor Day, the first Monday of the month. We honor working people on this day, usually limiting our celebration to rest and recreation.

There is no doubt that God expects us to work, to provide for ourselves and our families. "If a man will not work, he shall not eat" (2 Thessalonians 3:10). However, work, like anything else, can get out of focus. It can dominate all that a person thinks about or does to the extent that it throws everything else out of kilter.

Work may be one of society's few accepted addictions, yet it can be just as destructive as any other compulsive behavior. Workaholism destroys marriages, families, and the workaholic himself. Take an honest look at the way you approach your profession. If your job came to an end tomorrow, would you still have a reason to get up in the morning? Do you sometimes feel guilty, knowing you are putting work commitments ahead of family time? Can you forget about work when you are at home or on vacation? Do you have any health problems that may be work- or stress-related? Do you often bury yourself in work to escape from problems at home?

Take some time to think through your work habits. Discuss them and pray about them with your wife. Are there ways to adjust your schedule and outlook that will help you balance your work, family, and relaxation more appropriately? A person may even need to get professional help, because workaholism can be a means of hiding a myriad of deep-seated emotional problems. These problems can range from low self-esteem to sexual molestation. Through counseling, the person can unravel some of his emotional pain and move toward getting a better perspective on work.

A Secular View of Work

For many people, work identifies who they are, how successful they are, and what pleasures they can buy. Their very self-worth is determined by their success (or lack of success) at work. However, when a person builds his whole self-worth on his work or career, any setback in that area can be disastrous. For this reason, some people cannot handle the idea of retirement. Without work, their lives lose meaning. Worse yet, they can suffer a tragic spiritual consequence: "What good will it be for a man if he gains the whole world, yet forfeits his soul?" (Matthew 16:26). To make an idol of anything, including work, leaves God in second place (or simply out of the picture altogether).

God's Perspective on Work

What matters most to God is that the needs of His creation be met (Genesis 1:28; 2:8, 15). The greatest need was the salvation of humanity. God took care of that need by sending His Son, Jesus Christ, to die for our sins.

> *But in addition to salvation—obviously a need with eternal implications—mankind has many other needs. Just because many of them are temporal needs does not diminish their importance to God, nor does it diminish the value of the work done to meet those needs. In fact, God thinks they are important enough to equip a variety of people with various abilities to meet those needs. Furthermore, in meeting the legitimate needs of people, a worker is serving people who obviously have eternal value. In other words, the product of the work may be temporal but those who benefit from the work are eternal.*[25]

In other words, work is important, but it must be done to bring glory and honor to God, not to the one doing the work. Work has eternal implications. Through his work, a person loves God and others.

Keep Each Plate Spinning

The truth of the matter is this: No matter how hard we try, it's hard not to let our work become all-consuming and diminish the importance of our marriage and family. At times, all of us have to work at not letting our work enslave us. We must ask ourselves how much time we really *need* to spend at work. How much work is too much? We need to ask our wife and kids if our work load is hurting our relationship with them—and then truly listen to what they have to say. Is it really necessary to work overtime? Why am I working so many hours? Is my work hurting me physically or emotionally?

Many jobs do require an inordinate amount of time and energy. Some people simply have no choice if they want to keep their job and continue supporting their family. If this describes your situation, then you must use the time you do have with your family wisely. This means carefully scheduling any extra time with your wife and children. Your planning must be intentional, as when you make an important doctor's appointment. It means setting aside time for your family to play together, a time for just you and your wife to be alone, a time for that special birthday party.

Someone correctly said it, "Love is spelled T-I-M-E." Each year, the lives of your children grow more complex. There is increased peer pressure. There are more temptations and challenges, especially as they enter the teenage years. It's far easier to make a significant difference in the lives of your children if you do it from the beginning. This can only happen when you choose to set aside time to make a difference. At the end of their lives, few fathers regret not having worked harder. More regret not having spent more time with those they love the most—their family.

Dad Finds a Buddy

B. David Edens

Raymond Camp, who authored the column "Wood, Fish and Stream" for *The New York Times,* once received a letter from a boy. It read, "Would you tell me where I could find a place to fish that is not more than five or six miles from my home in Queens? I am fourteen years old and have saved up enough money to buy a rod, reel, and line, but do not know where to go fishing. My father goes almost every weekend, but he fishes with older men who don't want a boy along, so I have to find some place I can reach on my bicycle or the subway."

By resorting to the telephone directory, the columnist was able to obtain the father's name and sent him his son's letter with a brief note. He received this reply from the father, "You handed me quite a wallop in your letter, but I am sorry you did not hit me harder and sooner. When I think of the opportunity I might have lost, it frightens me. I do not need to point out that I now have a new fishing companion, and we have already planned a busy spring and summer. I wonder how many other fathers are passing up similar opportunities?"[26]

❧ Suggestions for Husbands ❧

Week 1

Spend the week examining your work.

➤ Ask your wife to evaluate your approach to your job.

➤ Compare her evaluation of your work to yours. Discuss the areas of disagreement. Make a plan to deal with any issues that need your attention.

➤ Someone said, "When I'm at work, I feel guilty that I'm not at home spending more time with my family. When I'm with my family, I feel guilty I'm not at work doing what I'm being paid for." Do you ever feel that way? If so, why? What's the solution? What do you think God would say about it? Talk to your wife about your thoughts.

➤ Look at the five main areas of your life: your work, your personal life, your family, your church, and your community. Which of the five areas suffer the most because of neglect on your part? What can you do about it? What *will* you do about it?

➤ Read the book *Your Work Matters to God* by Doug Sherman and William Hendricks (Navpress, 1993).

Week 2

Work on keeping *work* in proper perspective.

➤ Study what the Scriptures say about work (a concordance would prove helpful).

➤ Choose a new hobby and get started on it.

➤ Do your work in harmony with your values.

➤ Schedule a definite "come home" time each day.

➤ Park at the back of the parking lot at work. Then walk to your office. Physical exercise is good for you.

➤ Give your very best at work.

➤ Go to bed an hour early tonight.

➤ Play a game with your children and put as much energy into it as you do your work.

➤ When you see a stranded motorist, stop and ask if you can help.

Week 3

Work on spending more time with your wife.

➤ Take up a hobby your wife will enjoy doing with you.

➤ If you're a "night person" and she's a "day person" (or vice versa), try to adjust your body clock to fit hers.

➤ Do a "10-and-10"—10 minutes of talking to each other, 10 minutes of listening to each other.

➤ Pray with your wife.

➤ Be the first to say, "I love you."

➤ Take a cooking class together.

➤ Plant some flowers together.

➤ If your wife is usually making dinner when you get home from work, take over the preparations while she relaxes. At the very least, set the table.

Week 4

Work on making up a master calendar of events, scheduling different times to be with your wife and family.

➤ Decide on when and how you'd like to spend holidays, birthdays, and anniversaries. Start thinking about what you'd like to do, how you're going to afford it, etc.

➤ Schedule three to four weekends away for only you and your wife.

➤ Martin Luther said, "Let the wife make her husband glad to come home and let him make her sorry to see him leave." Discuss and write out some definite things you feel you can each do to assure that Luther's motto will become a reality in your home.

➤ If *love* is spelled T-I-M-E, what kind of grade would you receive in spelling? Agree on two or three things you can do to better spell *love* in your marriage.

➤ Schedule some time to be romantic.

➤ Suggestions for Fathers ➤

Week 1

Spend some time discussing work with your children (e.g., its purpose).

➤ If it's permitted, take your child along to work.

➤ Discuss the purpose of work according to God. Study Psalms 8 and 104.

➤ Discuss your family budget with your children.

➤ Ask your children for their reactions to your work schedule. Do they feel you spend too much time and energy on work and not enough on them? Do they see any problems with your attitude toward work? Make plans to address their concerns.

➤ Encourage your older children to get part-time jobs.

Week 2

Work on keeping *work* in proper perspective.

➤ Take up a hobby your children will enjoy doing with you.

➤ Pray with your children about the joys and concerns you have regarding your work.

➤ Join a gym with the whole family.

➤ Talk with your family about how you act when you first come home. How do your children see you (e.g., grumpy most of the time)? How would they like to see you? What would they like to do with you when you come home?

➤ Play a game of basketball together.

➤ Begin to exercise with the goal of taking two to three inches off your stomach. (If you're already trim, work instead on your cardiovascular system.)

➤ Think about the Scottish proverb: "Be a friend to yourself, and others will."

Week 3

Work on spending more time with your children.

➤ Go to a local football game this weekend.

➤ Pick up your child from school and go out for a special ice-cream sundae, just the two of you.

➤ Don't interrupt when your child talks to you.

➤ Go to the zoo.

➤ Learn the names of and something about your children's best friends.

➤ Give your children a point of reference by saying to them, "You are our special God-given children."

➤ Cherish your children for what they are as opposed to what you would like them to be.

➤ Prepare a meal together.

Week 4

Work on making a master calendar of events, scheduling different times to be with your family.

➤ Discuss with your children what they'd like to do on their next birthday. Schedule the days on your calendar.

➤ Plan a family vacation, getting your children's input.

➤ Since September is the beginning of the school year, review with your children their school calendars. Note what events they'd like you to attend (e.g., a special open house).

➤ Explain that some say *love* is spelled T-I-M-E. Ask your children how they think you're doing in spelling if the statement is true. Do they have any suggestions on how you might do better?

➤ Tell your children what you'd like them to do for you on your next birthday.

CELEBRATE YOUR FAITH STORY

It was one of those days that George Jaeger loved—a day of fishing with his three sons and his own father on the great Atlantic Ocean. By late afternoon, however, the day would turn nightmarish. First, when the group decided to head for shore, the boat's engine stalled. Then the winds suddenly kicked up and turned the mighty ocean into a ferocious enemy. The boat rocked back and forth helplessly on the water until it finally succumbed to the pounding waves. As it listed to the side, about to sink, George and his family had no choice but to jump into the icy waters with their life jackets and try to swim to shore. By 6:30 p.m. the boat had been swallowed by the angry sea.

Six-foot waves and a strong current made the swimming almost impossible. First one boy, and then another—and another ... swallowed too much water. Helpless, George Jaeger watched his sons and then his father die. Eight hours later, he staggered onto the shore, still pulling the rope that bound the bodies of the other four to him.

"I realized they were all dead—my three boys and my father—but I guess I didn't want to accept it, so I kept swimming all night long," he said to reporters. "My youngest boy, Clifford, was the first to go. I had always taught our children not to fear death because it was being with Jesus Christ. Before he died I heard him say, 'I'd rather be with Jesus than go on fighting.'"[27]

What could be more horrifying than watching your own children die before your very eyes? Only this: seeing them die without knowing Jesus Christ. George Jaeger had given his children the Word of eternal life. They died knowing that through the life, death, and resurrection of Jesus, they would be in heaven.

Performance under stress is one test of effective leadership. It may also be the proof of accomplishment when it comes to evaluating the quality of a father. In that awful Atlantic night, George Jaeger had a chance to see his three sons summon every ounce of the courage and self-control he had tried to build into them. The beautiful way they died said something about the kind of father George Jaeger had been for fifteen years.[28]

Everything a parent does pales in comparison with the great task of passing his faith on to the next generation. We can provide our children with the best education, the best physical care, the best financial opportunities, but we fail if we do not teach them the answer to life's ultimate question: What happens to me when I die?

Passing the Baton

Throughout Scripture God admonishes His people to pass the baton of faith on to the next generation:

> *These commandments that I give you today are to be upon your hearts. Impress them on your children. Talk about them when you sit at home and when you walk along the road, when you lie down and when you get up. Tie them as symbols on your hands and bind them on your foreheads. Write them on the door-frames of your houses and on your gates.* (Deuteronomy 6:6–9)

> *Therefore go and make disciples of all nations, baptizing them in the name of the Father and of the Son and of the Holy Spirit, and teaching them to obey everything I have commanded you.* (Matthew 28:19–20)

Passing on the faith might be compared to four-man teams competing in relay races. Each person on the team runs the same distance as the other three. After running the required distance, the person running passes a baton to the next teammate. Often, the races are won or lost by the way the baton is passed to the next runner. In a similar way, a child's faith can either be severely hampered or greatly aided by the way the baton is passed. When parents fail to pass the baton effectively or fail to pass it at all, they get in the way of the Holy Spirit. They "grieve the Holy Spirit" (Ephesians 4:30). They hinder Him from doing what He really wants to do in the lives of His people.

There was a little boy who fell out of bed in the middle of the night. When his father asked him what happened, he said, "I've really thought about that myself, and I think I have it all figured out. I must have stayed too close to where I got in." The same thing can happen to people with faith. They can stay too close to where they begin and fall out. (See Matthew 13:20–21.)

Passing on God's Love

In Jesus Christ, God became man, the perfect expression of the love of God for us. God's love is unconditional, undeserved, and everlasting. Through His Word and Holy Baptism, His love is poured into us by the Holy Spirit. It is this love that we reflect to our children and others.

Someone has said, "The best way for a father to love his children is to love their mother." If we fail to demonstrate this love, children may find it hard to believe that God is loving. It's important that we continually examine what kind of picture we are giving to our families about God's love. An examination might include such questions as these:

- Do I reflect an unconditional love for my family?

- Do I base my love on performance?

- Does my love waver or change depending on the circumstances?

- Do I love with forgiveness?

- Do I *behave* in love as opposed to just *being* in love?

- Do I love with praise and affirmation?

When asked what they think about God, here's what respondents said:

- Eighty-four percent think He is a heavenly Father reached by prayer.

- Five percent think He is an idea, not a being.

- Two percent think He is an impersonal Creator.

- Four percent don't know.

- Five percent don't believe in God or a universal spirit.[29]

Despite the fact that people had sinned and were not worthy of God's love, God loved them. Despite the fact that people crucified Jesus on the cross, the Son prayed, "Father, forgive them, for they do not know what they are doing" (Luke 23:34). Children can best love others when they know God loves them. The inspired writer said, "We love because He first loved us" (1 John 4:19). So much of what your children know about God's love will depend on you, their father. It will depend on how you reflect that love in your words and actions.

Teaching God's Values

There is much talk of "values" these days. Politicians—liberal and conservative—point to a "value's drought" in our country. The cover story of a recent issue of *Newsweek* was entitled "Shame: How Do We Bring Back a Sense of Right and Wrong?"[30] There is a tremendous urge to bring back a sense of right and wrong. The real question is this: How do we best do that?

Some people insist that you don't need to refer to God to teach values. This philosophy, obviously, is especially prevalent among atheists or agnostics. For instance, some baby boomers, those born between 1946 and 1964, grew up challenging many of the old traditional values, trying in the process to carve out their own basic values without reference to God. But I submit that it's impossible to teach children right from wrong without reference to God.

> *Morality without God is empty. ... It becomes purely subjective. ... What I say is good is good for me, and what Hitler says is good is good for him. ... Without God, morality becomes very pragmatic and relative. ... You can do things today, and deny them tomorrow based on what is popular or what benefits you personally. With God, there's a stable, fixed yardstick that makes a person accountable.*[31]

Christian parents do have a "yardstick" at their disposal—one they can use to fix the values they teach their children. It's called the Bible. God gives us parameters and boundaries for our own good. These principles and values—when carried out by us—bring Him glory and honor and benefit us and those around us greatly.

Each year, many Protestant churches set aside October 31 to celebrate the Reformation started by Martin Luther in Germany in 1517. While performing his daily task of teaching, Luther discovered from the Scriptures that, contrary to what he had been taught, people are justified before God by grace alone through faith in Christ alone, not through their good deeds.

> *For all have sinned and fall short of the glory of God, and are justified freely by His grace through the redemption that came by Christ Jesus. (Romans 3:23–24)*

Even though this is a biblical doctrine, it was considered a revolutionary thought—so much so that Luther was excommunicated from the Roman Catholic Church and placed under the ban of the Holy Roman emperor. He was made to fear for his life and forced repeatedly into hiding. When asked to withdraw his assertion that a person is justified by grace alone through faith alone, Luther simply said, "I cannot recant." He could not recant because what he believed was based on God's Word.

Sad to say, it's becoming more and more popular for Christians to compromise their values, to recant some of their ideas about what's right and wrong based on popular opinion or what the government or judicial system says is acceptable. A wise father will make sure that the values he teaches and holds to are those of God's Word. If not, he has no basis, no real foundation, for teaching his children.

Consider the idea of honesty. The need for honesty is clearly spelled out in Scripture, yet surveys tell us that 91 percent of Americans lie regularly. How many Christian men have recanted and compromised this important value to get ahead in business?

How about the important value of fidelity? How easy

is it to listen to the argument of a son or daughter—"But everyone is doing it, Dad!"—and then give in—compromising what you once confessed to have believed. Every father must remember Paul's clear instructions:

> *Do not conform any longer to the pattern of this world, but be transformed by the renewing of your mind. Then you will be able to test and approve what God's will is—His good, pleasing and perfect will. (Romans 12:2)*

━━━━●━━━━

Family Films of Concordia Publishing House has released a helpful video-based program called *Parenting with Values*. The program looks at six important values: responsibility, courage, respect, fidelity, compassion, and honesty. The course does more than identify important values; it actually describes important techniques to teach these values, including learning through experience and connecting your children with others who subscribe to the same values as you. In addition, the program suggests building blocks to help build each value.

Share Words of Eternal Life

In his gospel, John describes how some of Jesus' followers started leaving Him because they thought His teaching was too hard. When Jesus saw this happening, He asked the disciples: "You do not want to leave too, do you?" (John 6:67). Impetuous Simon Peter answered, "Lord, to whom shall we go? You have the words of eternal life. We believe and know that You are the Holy One of God" (John 6:68).

Simon Peter hit it right on the head when he said, "To whom shall we go?" There isn't anyone we can go to but Christ Jesus for the words of eternal life. There isn't any word from any educator, hero, or counselor that can tell our children the way to heaven. Only the words of Holy Scripture can do this.

Jesus said, "I am the way and the truth and the life. No one comes to the Father except through Me" (John 14:6). What will really matter in the end if your family—your wife, children, and grandchildren—don't know the way to heaven? It makes no difference if your daughter is elected the first woman president of the United States. When she closes her eyelids in death, all that will matter is if she knows the "words of eternal life." Your son may be the finest lawyer or athlete in the world, but in the end, all that will matter is if he trusts that Jesus Christ is His Savior. A father who teaches his children the words of life and death is the father who truly fulfills his God-given responsibility. A father who teaches his children how to die also teaches them how to live.

"Max, your dad's awake."

I had been watching a movie on TV. One of those thrillers that takes you from the here and now and transports you to the somewhere and sometime. My mother's statement seemed to come from another world. The real world.

I turned toward my father. He was looking at me.

His head was all he could turn. Lou Gehrig's disease had leeched his movement, taking from him everything but his faith ... and his eyes.

It was his eyes that called me to walk over to his bedside. I had been home for almost two weeks, on special leave from Brazil, due to his worsening condition. He had slept most of the last few days, awakening only when my mother would bathe him or clean his sheets.

Next to his bed was a respirator—a metronome of mortality that pushed air into his lungs through a hole in his throat. The bones in his hand protruded like spokes in an umbrella. His fingers, once firm and strong, were curled and lifeless. I sat on the edge of his bed and ran my hands over his barreled rib cage. I put my hand on his forehead. It was hot ... hot and damp. I stroked his hair.

"What is it, Dad?"

He wanted to say something. His eyes yearned. His eyes refused to release me. If I looked away for a moment, they followed me, and were still looking when I looked back.

"What is it?"

I'd seen that expression before. I was seven years old, eight at the most, standing on the edge of a diving board for the first time, wondering if I would survive the plunge. The board dipped under my seventy pounds. I looked behind me at the kids who were pestering me to hurry up and jump. I wondered what *they would do if I asked them to move over so I could get down. Tar and feather me, I supposed.*

So, caught between ridicule and a jump into certain death, I did the only thing I knew how to do—I shivered.

Then I heard him, "It's all right, son, come on in." I looked down. My father had dived in. He was treading water awaiting my jump. Even as I write, I can see his expression—tanned face, wet hair, broad smile, and bright eyes. His eyes were assuring and earnest. Had he not said a word, they would have conveyed the message. But he did speak. "Jump, it's all right."

So I jumped.

Twenty-three years later the tan was gone, the hair thin and the face drawn. But the eyes hadn't changed. They were bold. And their message hadn't changed. I knew what he was saying. Somehow he knew I was afraid. Somehow he perceived that I was shivering as I looked into the deep. And somehow, he, the dying, had the strength to comfort me, the living.

I placed my cheek in the hollow of his. My tears dripped on his hot face. I said softly what his throat wanted to, but couldn't. "It's all right," I whispered. "It's going to be all right."

When I raised my head, his eyes were closed. I would never see them open again.

He left me with a final look. One last statement of the eyes. One farewell message from the captain before

the boat would turn out to sea. One concluding
assurance from a father to a son, "It's all right."

❧ Suggestions for Husbands ❦

Week 1

Discuss with your wife how well you think you're passing the baton of faith to your children.

➤ Spend an evening on the porch or in front of the fireplace discussing how the baton of faith was passed to you (and your wife) by your parents.

➤ Study Deuteronomy 6:6–9. Assess how well you think you're doing in following this admonition. What things should you be doing to better carry it out?

➤ It is the Holy Spirit only who creates and sustains faith (1 Corinthians 2:14; 12:3). Knowing that the Holy Spirit works through the Word of God, spend some time discussing how your family might set aside more time for the study of God's Word.

➤ Study 2 Timothy 1:5. Then speak a prayer of thanks for those who passed the baton of faith to you for however many generations back you can recall.

➤ Make a video for your children. Include a testimony of what you believe about Jesus Christ, what you hope they will believe, and what you hope your children will pass down to their children some day.

Week 2

Share a picture of God's love with your wife this week.

➤ Send her a postcard or E-mail telling her, "I love you."

➤ Serve her breakfast in bed.

➤ Praise her in front of her parents.

➤ Take her wherever she would like to go (within reason, that is).

➤ Go canoeing, just the two of you. Stop somewhere on a sandy beach, away from people, and just talk.

➤ Read the newspaper together after you've made her favorite tea or coffee.

➤ Listen to your favorite kind of music together. Hold hands.

Week 3

Teach your children important values this week by valuing their mother.

➤ Sit down and look over your wedding pictures. In the presence of your children, tell your wife what your marriage vows mean to you.

➤ Spell out some ways your wife is dependable (e.g., she always gets everyone off to work or school in the morning). As you recall these things, praise her for them.

➤ Ask forgiveness for something you did or said that was dishonest.

➤ Brainstorm ways that you and your family obscure the facts with exaggerations, thus being dishonest (e.g., "You're never on time").

➤ Good body language tells the other person he or she matters. It shows respect for the other person. Make a point of looking people in the eyes today as you communicate. Also be sure the rest of your attending behavior is positive and warm.

➤ Pray with your wife that both of you might have teachable spirits.

Week 4

Share with your wife your fears and hopes about death.

➤ Read together 1 Corinthians 15, the great resurrection chapter.

➤ Share with each other specific requests about funeral arrangements you desire when you die (e.g., where to be buried). If you haven't already done so, write some of these requests down and put them in a place where those who are left to make your arrangements can find them.

➤ Discuss together where you think your children are in their relationship with Jesus Christ. End the discussion with a special prayer for your children.

➤ Memorize John 14:1–6.

➤ Go to the cemetery where your parents and/or grandparents are buried. Reflect on the things you remember about them, especially the things they believed in. While you're there, clean up around the grave site.

❧ Suggestions for Fathers ❧

Week 1

Creatively pass the baton of faith to your children this week.

➤ Sit down with your children and let them know how you would answer these two questions:

- What would happen to me if I were to die tonight? (One hopes your answer would include this thought, "I will go to heaven because Jesus Christ is my Savior.")

- If I should come before the gates of heaven and an angel of the Lord should ask, "Why should I let you in?" what would I say? (Answer: Let me in because of the blood of Jesus Christ, which redeemed me from sin, death, and the power of the devil.)

➤ Tell your children what you believe about the Holy Bible.

➤ Tell your children about your personal need for God's forgiveness and grace.

➤ Make sure your children catch you using your faith. Point out ways in which God is working in your children's lives.

➤ When you see the "little Gospel light" shining in your children, call their attention to it.

Week 2

Help your children see God's love through the love you share with them.

➤ Bring some special gift home for each child. Tell them it's just because you love them.

➤ Do your children's chores.

➤ Invite your children to tell you about their day. Look them in the eyes as they talk to you and listen very attentively!

➤ Deal with circumstances as they are, not as you wish they were.

➤ Specialize today in being an encourager.

➤ After your child has failed at something, remember that nobody wants to fail. They only fail because they don't know how to succeed. Make it your goal to teach them.

Week 3

Do at least one thing each day this week to teach the following values: responsibility, courage, respect, fidelity, compassion, and honesty.

➤ Make a conscientious effort this week to point out the responsibilities of those around you and the consequences of not carrying out those responsibilities (e.g., police officers, firefighters, doctors).

➤ Study Philippians 4:13 and its meaning for each

member of the family (e.g., "I can pass the test I've studied so hard for!").

➤ Study an age-appropriate book on manners.

➤ Play a game of "What Would You Do If ...?" (E.g., "... if someone brought a *Playboy* magazine to school?")

➤ Explain the meaning of the Chinese proverb: "Man stand for long time with mouth open before roast duck fly in."

➤ Pledge to show your children as much compassion as you show your closest friends or the people with whom you work.

➤ Go out of your way to praise your child whenever he or she, under difficult or inconvenient circumstances, tells the truth.

➤ Teach your children that a teenager who gets a girl pregnant is not a man, he's still a boy.

Week 4

Share with your children the assurance of heaven.

➤ Read to them the book *If I Should Die/If I Should Live* by Joanne Marxhausen (Concordia Publishing House, 1975).

➤ Memorize John 11:25.

➤ Recite this favorite children's prayer: "Now I lay me down to sleep. I pray the Lord my soul to keep. If I should die before I wake, I pray thee, Lord, my soul to take." Review what the prayer means, especially the fact that because of Jesus you can be assured that upon death your soul will be with the Lord in heaven.

➤ Sit down with your children and tell them why you know you're going to heaven someday. ("I'm going to heaven because I believe that Jesus Christ lived a perfect life for me. He died in my place and was resurrected from the dead, proving that the payment He had made was enough for my sins and the sins of the whole world.")

➤ Jesus promises us, "Because I live, you also will live" (John 14:19). Imagine with your children what heaven will be like. Talk about it using whatever picture language you think will be most helpful to them.

CELEBRATE SERVICE TO OTHERS

Our son, Jacob, was 2 years old when we first took him to the Los Angeles County Fair, the largest county fair in the world. Needless to say, he was quite excited when we told him he'd be seeing cows, riding a pony, and petting sheep and goats.

Upon arriving at the fair, Jacob immediately spotted a train. From that time on, we heard the same plea over and over, "Choo-choo train, Daddy … choo-choo train, Mommy."

His first train ride was great. He was alone, strapped into one of the open-air cars. With each circle the train made, he would put on a radiant smile and wave, almost as though he were in the movies, obediently following the director's cues.

On his next ride, we strapped him into the same car, but this time two other children, both slightly older than he, were strapped in alongside him.

One of the children obviously did not want to be on the train. As the engine started chugging again, tears cascaded down the boy's cheeks as he pleaded for release.

Jacob did not wave the first time around as he did before. He only looked at the crying boy.

The second time around, I feared he might start crying himself.

On the third circuit, he did something that almost brought tears to *my* eyes. He put his arm around the older boy, laid his head on the boy's shoulder, and tried as best he could to comfort him.

For a moment, it seemed to me that the cacophonous carnival calliope chimed out a new chord, one from Handel's *Messiah*, "Comfort ye My people, comfort ye, comfort ye My people, saith your God ..."

In a warm and wonderful way, Jacob reflected a picture of our heavenly Father, who puts His arm around us, lays His head on our shoulder, and comforts us. In compassion for His people, God sent His only Son, Jesus Christ, to die for us. And through that Son's life, death, and resurrection, this assurance is ours: "Though your sins are like scarlet, they shall be as white as snow; though they are red as crimson, they shall be like wool" (Isaiah 1:18).

Compassion on the Decline

Jacob was a toddler, yet he felt compassion for the stranger next to him. A survey recently showed that young people are twice as likely to volunteer to help others as adults; however, volunteering in general has declined significantly in the last five years. An Independent Sector's survey indicated that 54 percent of the population in 1989 did some form of volunteer work compared with 48 percent in 1993.

Such surveys should not surprise us. As people

become more self-centered and less God-centered, they become less and less concerned about others. Paul describes people who distance themselves from God.

> *For although they knew God, they neither glorified Him as God nor gave thanks to Him, but their thinking became futile and their foolish hearts were darkened. ...*

> *Therefore God gave them over in the sinful desires of their hearts to sexual impurity for the degrading of their bodies with one another. They exchanged the truth of God for a lie, and worshiped and served created things rather than the Creator— who is forever praised. Amen. ...*

> *They have become filled with every kind of wickedness, evil, greed and depravity. ... They are senseless, faithless, heartless, ruthless. (Romans 1:21, 24–25, 29, 31)*

When a person is no longer connected vertically with God, he or she is unable to connect horizontally with others. Such a person becomes self-centered, caring only about "me, myself, and I." The Golden Rule, "Do to others what you would have them do to you" (Matthew 7:12), changes to, "Use others to get what you need." In a world that cares so little for caring, it's hard to raise children with servants' hearts. Servants' hearts do not come about naturally but only by the Holy Spirit's power.

A Commandment to Love

Jesus makes it clear that love is not optional.

"A new command I give you: Love one another. As I have loved you, so you must love one another. By this all men will know that you are My disciples, if you love one another." (John 13:34–35)

Love is not a suggestion. It's a commandment. The commandment to love was already known in Old Testament times. Our ability to love others is derived from the love that Jesus displayed through His death on the cross. Loving others is the distinguishing mark of Jesus' disciples. It summarizes the whole of God's teaching about how we should treat one another.

Love is the primary witness of who we are and to whom we belong—the Lord Jesus Christ. Steve Sjogren in his book *Conspiracy of Kindness* suggests that God uses acts of kindness shown by His people to convince others of His love. Sjogren calls this "servant evangelism." He defines it as "demonstrating the kindness of God by offering to do some act of humble service with no strings attached."[32] Such acts of kindness paint a picture of the grace of God—free and without strings attached.

The Strings That Hamper Servanthood

Though God's grace comes with no strings attached, we often attach strings to our servanthood.

- "I'll help, but not right now. I'm busy."
- "It's too risky for me to stop and help."
- "What's in it for me?"
- "They got themselves into that mess. Let them get themselves out of it."

Though some of these concerns may be legitimate at times, more often than not they serve only as excuses for not showing kindness. Jesus never counted the cost of being a servant. He risked all, even His life, to serve His people.

> Your attitude should be the same as that of Christ Jesus: Who, being in very nature God, did not consider equality with God something to be grasped, but made Himself nothing, taking the very nature of a servant, being made in human likeness. And being found in appearance as a man, He humbled Himself and became obedient to death—even death on a cross!" (Philippians 2:5–8)

Beginnings Are Sometimes Very Small

People often think of servanthood as doing something grand— like working alongside former President Jimmy Carter in building houses for the poor or serving hot meals every Saturday at the homeless shelter. The fact is, however, most people develop a servant's heart with very small beginnings, when they are very young. They start sharing with others in small ways. It may be giving away toys or clothes they've outgrown. It may be a special patch of flowers they raise just to give to people who need encouragement. These things prepare them to be generous in bigger ways later.

Pictures of Servanthood

Servanthood can be seen in many different forms and shapes.

- Ed's illness sometimes makes his pain unbearable. Unfortunately, he often takes his frustration out on his wife. People call her a saint because no matter how disrespectful Ed is to her, she always speaks kindly to him and treats him with great respect.

- John and his family were driving to the beach. The weather was hot and muggy. At times, traffic came to a standstill. When John saw two elderly Chinese people pull over to the edge of the freeway with smoke spewing from their car, he stopped to help, despite the protests of his family.

- Chuck and Denise decided to give an open invitation to anyone in their congregation who did not have somewhere to go for Thanksgiving dinner to come to their house. They were surprised at the number of people who responded.

- Robin insists that Jacob first write a thank-you note to each person outside the immediate family who has given him a Christmas gift before he plays with the gift. The note also must include a line or two about why he appreciates the gift.

- Marsha is a single mother. Her next-door neighbors often volunteer to baby-sit her children so she can have a night off.

- Grandma Jones is a 94-year-old invalid. She tells her friends, "I can't do much as far as preparing a meal for those who come home from the hospital or from a funeral, but I can pray. Every day I pray for those on the prayer list in the church bulletin."

Teaching Kindness by Example

It's no secret that children learn from observing others, especially their parents. Children will learn to value the things you value. They will walk the walk you walk. If they see you treat people with kindness, they'll treat others with kindness. They will learn to be more generous and helpful. Remember, "an acorn does not fall far from the branch."

> *There are little eyes upon you*
> *and they're watching night and day;*
> *there are little ears that quickly*
> *take in every word you say;*
> *there are little hands all eager*
> *to do anything you do;*
> *and little fellows dreaming*
> *of the day they'll be like you.*[33]

It should be the desire of every father, with the Holy Spirit's help, to instill in his child a servant's heart. Helping a child develop such a heart, encouraging him to show kindness to others, brings glory and honor to God and helps the child become a happier, more fulfilled person. This, in turn, helps society. If we have any doubt about what such a heart looks like, we need only review what Paul tells us in Philippians 2:3–4:

> *Do nothing out of selfish ambition or vain conceit, but in humility consider others better than yourselves. Each of you should look not only to your own interests, but also to the interests of others.*

❯❯ Suggestions for Husbands ❮❮

Week 1

Study with your wife key Bible stories and verses that speak of servanthood.

➤ "I planted the seed, Apollos watered it, but God made it grow" (1 Corinthians 3:6). Note how faith grows. Remember God speaks to you through His holy Word. How much time are you spending in it each week?

➤ Study John 13:1–17. What kinds of things can you do for each other this week that will be a form of washing each other's feet?

➤ Study 1 Samuel 12:23; Colossians 1:9; and James 5:16. What do these verses say about the importance of praying for one another? How often do you pray for each other as husband and wife?

➤ Pray 1 Peter 4:8–11.

➤ Study Philippians 2:3–8. How might things change between you and your spouse if you applied these words to your marriage?

➤ Memorize John 13:34–35.

Week 2

Display God's grace with no strings attached.

➤ Forgive your wife without any conditions for something hurtful she's said.

- Without any derogatory comments, help your wife get out of a mess she's gotten herself into.

- Go through an entire day without being critical of your wife or your kids.

- Clean the bathrooms. See if your wife notices what you did. If not, don't say a word.

- When your wife comes to the dinner table, stand up and pull out her chair.

- Open the car door for your wife.

Week 3

Brainstorm ways in which you can creatively celebrate Thanksgiving.

- Invite someone to your home who would normally be alone on Thanksgiving Day to celebrate with your family.

- Select five people who have been important to your family this last year. Send each of these people a homemade card filled with messages from each member of the family.

- The Pilgrims placed a kernel of corn on their Thanksgiving dinner plates to remind them that a small amount of corn helped them survive the terrible winter of the past year. Place three kernels of corn on each person's plate and ask them to place one kernel at a time in a large basket. As they do, ask them to tell three different things they are specifically thankful for.

➤ Offer to help serve Thanksgiving dinner at a local homeless shelter.

➤ Don't watch any football games on Thanksgiving Day. Instead, do whatever your wife would like to do.

Week 4

Practice servanthood in your community this week.

➤ If you know a single mom, have your wife and kids take her and her children out for ice cream while you change the oil in her car.

➤ Take in your neighbor's garbage cans.

➤ Rake an elderly neighbor's leaves.

➤ Go to your local park and pick up trash.

➤ Visit someone who has just lost a spouse. How about inviting that person over for dinner?

❥ Suggestions for Fathers ❦

Week 1

Study with your children Bible stories and verses that speak of servanthood.

➤ Memorize John 15:13.

➤ Study the story of the good Samaritan (Luke 10:25–37). Ask your children to identify people they know of who have special needs, like those of the man who was been beaten on the road to Jericho.

➤ Recite John 3:16. As you do, place each child's name in the blank space: "For God so loved _____ that He gave His one and only Son, that _____ [who] believes in Him shall not perish but have eternal life."

➤ Study passages that speak of kindness: John 13:35; Romans 12:15; 1 Corinthians 13:4–8; Ephesians 4:32.

➤ Discuss how the kindness the Holy Spirit produces in each of us is one way God answers other peoples' prayers. See also Matthew 25:40.

➤ Study Exodus 17:8–13. Point out how Aaron and Hur's helpfulness helped win the battle. Ask your children to identify someone they might help who is struggling with a difficult situation.

Week 2

Display God's grace, grace with no strings attached.

➣ Forgive your children for something they did without imposing any consequences, such as a time-out.

➣ Identify someone in your children's school who is not liked by very many people. Encourage your children to invite this person to play ball with you or to see a movie.

➣ Buy a special gift for your child for no other reason than to say, "I love you."

➣ Help your children do something they hate to do, such as dry the dishes.

➣ Make your child's bed.

➣ Whisper a few encouraging words into the ears of your children this evening before they go to sleep. Then when they awaken in the morning, they'll get up with happy words still ringing in their ears.

➣ Buy a special gift for your child that is something for life, such as an antique bed or desk.

➣ Explain to your children the meaning of Mark Twain's statement, "He liked to like people; therefore, people liked him."

Week 3

In the week when we normally give thanks to God for His many blessings, help your children see ways they can share those bountiful blessings with others.

➣ Take your child along to help you serve meals at a homeless shelter.

➤ Help select a special Thanksgiving Day card for Mom. Encourage each child to write his or her own personal message in the card.

➤ Buy some candy or get a gift certificate to a local restaurant and give it to your mail carrier. Tell him or her that you know the next month will be a very busy one with Christmas just around the corner.

➤ After eating Thanksgiving dinner, wash the dishes with your children and let Mom rest.

Week 4

Do some community activity with your children this week. Make sure the service projects are simple and safe for the child to participate in. It's important that their first experiences be positive.

➤ Go to the park and pick up trash.

➤ Wash someone's car for free.

➤ Collect aluminum cans. Cash them in and give the money to someone in need.

➤ Help an elderly person cross the street.

➤ Bake a cake and take it to your local fire station.

CELEBRATE TRADITIONS

There is a poignant story about a devout Christian man and his cat. The man would religiously devote one hour each day to meditation and prayer. He would always spend this sacred time in his bedroom because it was the quietest place in the house. The man looked forward to this special time every day. So did his cat because during this time the cat would snuggle next to him, purr, and receive loving strokes from his master. Soon, however, the man noticed that the cat seemed to demand more of his attention and was actually distracting him from concentrating on his Bible study and prayers, so he tied the cat to the bedpost.

The man's son noticed how helpful this time was for his father. When he moved out of the house into his own home, he wanted to implement the same meditative practices. So just as he'd seen his father do, he went to his bedroom, tied up his cat, and communed for one hour with God. But then the children came along. His job became more demanding, and he seemed to have less and less time for meditation. So the man simply spent 15 minutes each day having devotions.

When that man's daughter grew up and married, she decided she wanted to follow some of her family's traditions, especially the time alone in the bedroom. But for her the pace of life had quickened even more than for her father. After all, her house payment was five times greater than what he had ever paid. She had two children who always seemed to have either a soccer or a T-ball game. Her husband traveled a great deal and wasn't home many nights to help with the children. She just never seemed to have any spare time. Nevertheless, she was dedicated to following some of her parents' and grandparents' traditions. So she simply tied the cat to the bedpost each day for a short while and forgot about spending any time in prayer and meditation.

Many people celebrate Christmas in like manner. They buy presents, trim the tree, give grand parties—or "tie the cat to the bedpost"—but forget the real reason for the celebration. They retain some of the tradition but forget the reason behind it. Thus, they miss the most important part of the celebration.

The true meaning of such holidays as Christmas, Easter, Thanksgiving, and All Saints' Day (the day after Halloween) have been all but lost in our secularized society. The baby Jesus in the manger has long since been replaced by Santa in the chimney. The risen Lord has been exchanged for a chocolate Easter bunny. The exclamation "Thanksgiving Day!" has been downgraded to "Turkey Day!"

Christians need to hold true to the real reasons for special holidays, or "holy days." They need to focus on the real reason for Christmas and Easter, for St. Valentine's Day and Thanksgiving Day. Through traditions, Christian families can celebrate holidays with a greater zeal and excitement than anyone else because they know the true significance of these occasions.

Family Traditions

When a family does certain things in the same way enough times, it becomes a tradition. For this reason, you often hear members of a family say, "It just wouldn't be Christmas without it"—"it" being a certain Christmas tradition. Such a tradition might be going as a family into the forest and chopping down a Christmas tree. For those of Scandinavian descent, it might mean making lefse and krumkakke together, using the same tins that Great-Grandma used.

In a real sense, traditions become part of a legacy passed down from one generation to the next. Each family has its own library of legacies—a library that keeps the generations connected.

Traditions Established by God

God taught His people to celebrate important events. Note the Festival of the Passover that celebrates the independence of the Israelites from Egyptian domination. "For the generations to come you shall celebrate [Passover] as a festival to the LORD—a lasting ordinance" (Exodus 12:14).

Pharaoh had refused to let the Israelites leave Egypt. The reason was obvious: the Hebrews were cheap labor. They had become the Egyptians' slaves. Plague after plague had failed to convince the Pharaoh to let God's people go. With the 10th plague, however, he was finally convinced. The Israelites were told to splatter the blood of a lamb or a kid on the sides and top of their doorframes. The meat of the sacrificed animal was to be roasted and eaten along with bitter herbs and unleavened bread. That night, the angel of death passed over the homes of those who had blood on their door frames, but it struck dead the firstborn sons of Egyptian homes. From that time on, the Israelites were instructed to celebrate their deliverance for seven days each year (Exodus 12:14–16).

Each aspect of the Passover had special meaning for its celebrants. The slaughtered lamb or kid reminded them of God's protection of and provision for His people. The bitter herbs reminded them of their persecution and suffering in Egypt. The unleavened bread reminded them of their quick departure from Egypt. The Passover meal, year after year, generation after generation, reminded the people of how God had kept His promises to them. It reminded them that they were, indeed, His chosen people, set aside to be the people of the Savior.

Just as the Israelites were reminded of God's faithfulness through the celebration of Passover, so we are reminded of God's faithfulness in different festivals throughout the year—Christmas, Easter, Pentecost. In the seasons of Advent and Lent, we have the opportunity to retell our families the story of God's faithfulness—a God who sent a Savior to redeem a faithless and adulterous people from sin, death, and the power of the devil. We can also use other special days—birthdays, wedding anniversaries, baptismal birthdays—as special opportunities to talk to our children about God's love and faithfulness.

Traditions Are Not Instantaneous

We live in a day and age when everything is instant or microwavable. We are bombarded with talk about 80,000 megabytes and instant coverage of events 5,000 miles away. Out of this comes the myth that we can produce memories and cherished traditions overnight. But memories and traditions are built with lots of hard work and time. A tradition is built when a family intentionally goes out and cuts their Christmas tree rather than buying one off the lot. A tradition is formed when a father takes his daughter out every Sunday evening for her favorite ice cream instead of vegetating in front of the TV. A tradition is acquired when a father camps out in the woods with his kids, despite the fact that a motel room would seem much more comfortable. Creating a tradition means *making* family activities a priority on the family calendar. It means grabbing those one-on-one opportunities to bond with your children.

Preparation for Celebration

There's a saying, "If you fail to plan, plan to fail." Much of our failure to truly celebrate the various holidays derives from our failure to properly plan for them. We can learn a valuable lesson from the early Christian church whose members often spent weeks preparing for the special events of Christmas and Easter. Some churches still encourage such preparation by holding special services and studies. More and more often, however, these churches are finding fewer people eager to take advantage of these opportunities.

We celebrate Christ's birth on December 25. Some churches hold special midweek services—Advent services—during the four weeks leading up to the 25th. These services help worshipers prepare for the festival of Christmas, even as John the Baptist urged people to prepare for the coming of the Christ, "Repent, for the kingdom of heaven is near" (Matthew 3:2).

Extending the celebration of Christmas over a longer period of time helps us stay focused on the real reason for the celebration. There are more on-the-spot teachable moments to help underscore the real meaning of the holy day. You don't have to try to make it all happen in one day. Even if you did try, there would almost certainly be a dozen other activities to distract your children on Christmas Day.

The Secret Is in the Sharing

Memories are made by people sharing experiences. Your children are more likely to remember the times you did things *with* them as opposed to the times you merely talked *to* them. These shared experiences do not even have to be positive.

When my son was only 2 years old, he loved the

lights of Christmas and was always impressed with the neighbors' outdoor lights. Night after night, he would point to them, saying, "Lights, Daddy, lights."

Why, I thought, if my Jewish and Buddhist neighbors could string such an array of lights that so impressed my son, certainly I could and should do even more. After all, we, the across-the-street Christians, had something to say to them and to all passersby! Jesus has come to be the light of the world.

So Uncle Doug and I took an afternoon off and began the tedious process of stringing lights. Up and down we floated on the ladder, winding the lights from one corner of the house to the next.

In daylight the lights seemed to work perfectly, but the grand premiere would have to wait till night. When darkness had fallen, I gathered my wife, our houseguest, and of course, the one person I knew would be most impressed, Jacob, in front of the house. I pushed the magical plug into the socket. Expecting to hear oohs and aahs, all I heard was "Honey, are you sure you've plugged it in?"

After working frantically on it, I was able to get a short string to start glowing.

"*More* lights Daddy … *more* lights," Jacob said as he pointed to the home of our Buddhist neighbor.

All the Jacobs of the world need to see "more lights" because "darkness covers the earth and thick darkness is over the peoples" (Isaiah 60:2).

Jacob is now 7 years old, and we still talk about that memorable experience. Every year as I climb the ladder and Jacob hands me the strings of lights, I remind him of the first lighting attempt. We laugh and then dream about how much grander and better this year's lights will be than last year's. The shared experience of that first lighting, even though it was largely a dud, has built for us a memory and a tradition.

Make it one of your goals to create loving, lasting memories for your family. A good time to start is now, in the month we celebrate the holy day of Christmas—when "the Word became flesh and made His dwelling among us" (John 1:14). In so doing, you will be sharing who you are and the knowledge of the one to whom you belong, not only with the next generation but with many generations to come.

❧ Suggestions for Husbands ❧

Week 1

This week, review the family memories and traditions you and your wife remember from your childhoods.

➤ Discuss your favorite memories and traditions of Christmas. Ask, *Which traditions would we like to make sure to pass on to our children? Which would we not like passed on? Why?*

➤ Discuss memories and traditions of Easter. Ask, *Which traditions would we like to make sure to pass on to our children? Which would we not like passed on? Why?*

➤ Discuss memories of birthday parties. Are there some similar things you'd like to do for your children when they celebrate their birthdays?

➤ Discuss ways in which your families celebrated Halloween. What would you like to change about the way your children celebrate this day? Look up *Halloween* in an encyclopedia and find out how it originated. (Note that the word means "hallowed, or holy, evening." It was so named because it took place before All Saints' Day, which honored the saints who passed on.) How can you make Halloween more *hallowed* for your children?

➤ Study the reasons why some people celebrate the six weeks prior to Easter in a season called Lent and four weeks before Christmas in a period they call Advent. How would such celebrations help your family? If you are already observing these times of the year, how might they become even more meaningful for your family?

Week 2

Study the events leading up to Christmas to enhance your Christmas celebration.

➤ Study Luke 1:26–56 and Matthew 1:18–25. Talk about the obedience and trust of both Mary and Joseph.

➤ C. S. Lewis said, "Christianity has no message for those who do not realize they are sinners." Do you agree or disagree with this statement? Review the angel's announcement in Luke 2:11.

➤ Review Old Testament prophecies and their fulfillment according to the New Testament: Micah 5:2/Matthew 2:1; Psalm 72:10/Matthew 2:1, 11; Jeremiah 31:15/Matthew 2:16; Isaiah 7:14/Matthew 1:23.

➤ Listen to Handel's *Messiah*. As you do, look up some of the key passages used as follows:
Part 1: Isaiah 40:1–5; Haggai 2:6–7; Malachi 3:1–3; Isaiah 7:14; Isaiah 40:9; Isaiah 60:2–3; Isaiah 50:13; Isaiah 9:2, 6; Luke 2:8–14; Zechariah 9:9–10; Isaiah 35:5–6; Isaiah 40:11; Matthew 11:28–30.
Part 2: John 1:29; Isaiah 53:3; Isaiah 50:6; Isaiah 53:4–6; Psalm 22:7–8; Psalm 69:20; Lamentations 1:12; Isaiah 53:8; Psalm 16:10; Psalm 24:7–10; Hebrews 1:5–6; Psalm 68:18; Psalm 68:11; Romans 10:15, 18; Psalm 2:1–4, 9; Revelation 19:6; Revelation 11:15; Revelation 19:16.

Part 3: Job 19:25–26; 1 Corinthians 15:20–22, 51–57; Romans 8:31, 33–34; Revelation 5:12–13.

➤ Read Mark 1:1–5 for a helpful suggestion on how you can better prepare for the celebration of Jesus' birth.

Week 3

Build some Christmas memories this year by doing some special things.

➤ Decorate your Christmas tree in a different way. Try a Christian custom going back to the 13th century: Decorate it with 33 white roses, symbolizing the 33 years of Christ's earthly ministry and how He became the Rose of Sharon for us (Song of Songs 2:1; Isaiah 35:1). Intertwine a white streamer among the branches, symbolizing God's promise, "Though your sins are like scarlet, they shall be as white as snow" (Isaiah 1:18).

➤ Go caroling through your neighborhood.

➤ Fall down in the snow and make angels by sliding your arms up and down. Talk about how angels announced the Good News of Christmas (Luke 2:9–14).

➤ Read the Christmas story every night this week in front of a fireplace or in some other comfortable area. Give each member of the family his or her turn to read it on a particular day of the week. Use a children's Bible for those who are younger.

➤ Share the gifts you have as husband and wife before Christmas Eve so that on Christmas Day (or whenever you open the other presents), you can give full attention to the others.

Week 4

Work on continuing the celebration of Christmas.

➤ Host an after-Christmas slumber party for some of your favorite relatives, both children and adults. Sing Christmas carols. Eat! Have fun. Read the Christmas story late at night. Give each person a votive candle and light them as someone reads Matthew 4:16.

➤ Go throughout the neighborhood doing neighborly things and leaving a note saying, "Merry Christmas!" (e.g., shoveling snow out of a neighbor's driveway).

➤ Think of three gifts you could give to someone who didn't have a very merry Christmas. The three gifts symbolize the gifts of the Wise Men to the Christ Child—gold, frankincense, and myrrh (Matthew 2:11).

➤ Read the story of the visit of the Magi (Matthew 2:1–12). Just as the Wise Men returned home changed, ask in what ways Christmas has changed you and your family.

➤ Psychologists talk about the "post-holiday blues." Keep that from happening in your home by reminding each other daily of the Christmas promises. Take an empty prescription bottle and label it "Prescription for the post-Christmas blues. Take as needed!" Write 20 special Christmas promises, one each on a slip of paper approximately three inches by a half inch. Place the bottle in a convenient location and take as needed.

⤜ Suggestions for Fathers ⤛

Week 1

Begin making some special Christmas memories with your children.

➤ Share with your children a favorite memory of what you and your father used to do during the Christmas season. Then ask them if they would like to do the same thing. If so, do it.

➤ Instead of *buying* a Christmas tree, schedule a time when you can go and chop one down yourself. Make sure each child has a part in this important memory-building activity.

➤ Teach your children one of the Christmas songs your parents taught you when you were little.

➤ Go shopping early in the season to buy a special gift for Mom. Promise to keep quiet about what you bought.

➤ Turn off the TV and sit around the fireplace discussing what everyone would like Christmas to look, smell, and feel like this year.

Week 2

Study the scriptural accounts leading up to Christmas and the event itself.

➤ As a family, memorize Luke 2:1–20. Then go out caroling and recite the words between the music.

- Study the following verses: Isaiah 53:6; 59:2; John 3:16; John 1:29; 1 John 4:9. Discuss why Jesus came to earth.

- Study Jesus, the Messiah, according to the prophet Isaiah in Isaiah 7:14; 9:6–7; 11:1–3; 40:11; 49:6; and 53:3–6.

- Study Luke 1:29–38. Role-play the story. Ask one child to make whatever sounds might be heard throughout the story. Ask another to be the angel and your wife to be Mary.

- For your family prayer, memorize and sing together stanza 3 of "Away in a Manger."

Week 3

Build some Christmas memories for your children this year by doing some special things.

- Make a Christmas memory book with your children.

- Put an electric or battery-operated candle in each of your front windows as a reminder to your neighbors that Christ's coming on Christmas brings light to a world in darkness.

- Take a gift to someone who won't get any other gift during this Christmas season.

- Read the conclusion of the Christmas story in Matthew 28:1–10.

- Send a secret note to someone who needs encouragement. Don't sign your name; just wish him or her a very merry Christmas and say you're thinking about him or her.

➤ Take your children to a performance of the *Messiah*.

➤ Make up Christmas service cards for every member of the family. These cards might say things like this: "This card entitles you to a free car wash." Ask each member of the family to make up several cards for the other family members. Exchange these service cards as gifts. They can be redeemed anytime within the next year. In this way, the spirit of Christmas giving continues throughout the year.

Week 4

Use this last week of December to review with your children how well you've done as their father over the last year.

➤ Consider forgiveness—yours and theirs. Are there some wrongs that you've done against your children or that they've done against you that still need resolving? Practice confession and forgiveness.

➤ Consider commitment. Have you kept the promises you've made to your children? If not, what needs to happen?

➤ Consider responsibility. Discuss with the children ways that you would like them to become more responsible. Let them tell you what kinds of things they feel would help them to become more responsible.

➤ Consider time. Review your calendar once again, noting the special occasions such as vacations and birthdays that you have planned as a family. Dream a little together about these fun times.

➤ Consider how you've shared your faith with your children. In what way do you hope you'll do that better in the coming year? Do they know the answer to life's ultimate question: What happens to me when I die?

➤ Consider your service to others. Have you helped your children develop more servant-like hearts over the past year? If not, how can you do a better job in the coming year?

➤ Ask each member of the family to make a list of resolutions. Then write them out on poster board and post the list somewhere conspicuous. End with prayer that God will help you keep these resolutions.

NOTES

1. Gary Smalley and John Trent, *The Blessing* (New York: Pocket Books, 1986), 27.

2. Nancy Ross-Flanigan, "The Power of Touch," *Pasadena Star-News* (April 24, 1995), section 5.

3. Smalley and Trent, 96.

4. Quoted from an unknown source.

5. A. C. Green, *Victory* (Orlando: Creation House, 1994), 157–58.

6. Ruth Harms Calkin, *Marriage Is So Much More, Lord* (Wheaton: Tyndale House Publishers, 1979), 33.

7. Roger Sonnenberg and David J. Ludwig, *Living with Purpose* (St. Louis: Family Films, 1994), 93.

8. Richard J. Foster, *Prayer: Finding the Heart's True Home* (San Francisco: Harper San Francisco, 1992), 3–4.

9. George Gallup Jr. and Sarah Jones, *100 Questions and Answers: Religion in America* (Princeton, NJ: Princeton Religion Research Center, 1984), 38.

10. C. S. Lewis, *Letters to Malcom: Chiefly on Prayer* (New York: Harcourt, Brace, & World, 1964), 91.

11. Green, 142.

12. Dietrich Bonhoeffer, *Life Together* (New York: Harper & Row, 1952), 112.

13. Author unknown.

14. *Hymns for the Living Church* (Carol Stream, IL: Hope Publishing Company, 1977), 569.

15. Roger Sonnenberg, *Preparation for a Celebration* (St. Louis: Concordia Publishing House, 1990), 29.

16. Corrie ten Boom, "I'm Still Learning to Forgive," *Guideposts*, 1972.

17. Roger Sonnenberg, *Parenting with Purpose*, Participant's Worksheets (St. Louis: Family Films, 1992), session 6, pages 1–2.

18. Lewis B. Smedes, *Caring and Commitment* (San Francisco: Harper & Row, 1989), 92.

19. *Christian Science Monitor*, September 5, 1978, 28.

20. Nick Stinnett and John DeFrain, "Six Secrets of Strong Families," *Reader's Digest*, November 1987, 133.

21. Claire Berman, *A Hole in My Heart: Adult Children of Divorce Speak Out* (New York: Simon and Schuster, 1992), 18.

22. M. Scott Peck, *The Road Less Traveled* (New York: Simon and Schuster, 1978), 140–41.

23. Charles R. Swindoll, *Come before Winter and Share My Hope* (Grand Rapids: Zondervan Publishing House, 1985), 233–35.

24. Carl Spackman, *Parents Passing On the Faith* (Wheaton, IL: Victor Books, 1989), 42.

25. Doug Sherman and William Hendricks, *Your Work Matters to God* (Colorado Springs: Navpress, 1993), 53.

26. B. David Edens, "Dad Finds a Buddy," *Father with Love* (Nashville: Dimensions for Living, 1995), 100.

27. Gordon MacDonald, *The Effective Father* (Wheaton, IL: Tyndale House Publishers, 1977), 14.

28. Ibid, 14.

29. Gallup Jr. and Jones, 4.

30. *Newsweek*, February 6, 1995.

31. Roy Rivenburg, "No Need for God?" *Los Angeles Times* (June 10, 1993), E5.

32. Steve Sjogren, *Conspiracy of Kindness* (Ann Arbor, MI: Servant Publications, 1993), 17–18.

33. Joe White, *What Kids Wish Parents Knew about Parenting* (Sisters, OR: Questar Publishers, 1988), 187.